Thoughts for Men on the Move

Thoughts for Men on the Move

by

Warren W. Wiersbe

MOODY PRESS
CHICAGO

© 1970, 1988 by
THE MOODY BIBLE INSTITUTE
OF CHICAGO

Expanded Paperback Edition, 1988

ISBN: 0-8024-8781-5

2 3 4 5 6 Printing/LC/Year 93 92 91 90 89

For my wife, Betty, whose love and encouragement have always given added strength for the journey

Preface

This little book of meditations is an attempt to help Christian men find spiritual strength from the Word of God.

How our churches need men of God today! Men who love the Word and obey it; men who have a burden for souls and seek to win them to Christ; men who fear God, hate sin, and lead their families forward in the will of God.

This book is not a substitute for your Bible. Neither is it a substitute for your own personal meditation on the Word of God. Rather, it is an encouragement for systematic Bible reading and prayer, an illustration of what God can say to us if we will but listen.

Each of these meditations grew out of my own daily time with the Lord. Most of them were originally published in my earlier book *Byways of Blessing* and, at the request of the publishers, were completely rewritten for this book.

They have been a blessing and help to me and to men with whom I have shared them. I trust they will also be a help to you and give you additional strength for the journey.

Strength for the Journey

Whether a man carries a briefcase or a lunch bucket, he needs strength for the journey.

Elijah had been in hiding for three years when God called him to face the Baal worshipers on Mount Carmel. Because he had been waiting on the Lord, Elijah was able to "mount up with wings" and overcome the enemy.

In fact, 1 Kings 18:46 informs us that the prophet was able to run and not be weary as he raced ahead of the king's chariot!

But when it came to his day-by-day walk, Elijah discovered that the journey was "too great" for him. He became discouraged and wearied and finally had to quit.

Only God can give a man strength for the journey. Not the journey of a lifetime, or even the journey of a week. "As thy days, so shall thy strength be," God promises us in Deuteronomy 33:25. As the hymn writer put it,

> Day by day and with each passing moment,
> Strength I find to meet my trials here;
> Trusting in my Father's wise bestowment,
> I've no cause for worry or for fear.

The strength for the journey comes when we wait before the Lord at the beginning of the day. It comes from meditation and prayer, worship and surrender. It comes when a man spends time in God's Word before the day begins. Yes, you need strength for the journey, and God will graciously meet that need—if you let Him.

God Is Sufficient!

Paul asks a personal question in 2 Corinthians 2:16: "Who is sufficient for these things?" By "these things" the apostle means the demands and sacrifices of the Christian life. Who is sufficient for living a creative, victorious Christian life?

But Paul does more than ask the question; *he gives us the answer!* "Our sufficiency is of God" (3:5). We have no power of our own, no wisdom of our own; but we belong to the One who is the very power and wisdom of God!

Christ is sufficient for a man's spiritual needs. We draw upon His fullness of grace, according to John 1:16; and Philippians 4:13 declares that the believer can "do all things through Christ" who strengthens him. Because you are united to Christ, His spiritual resources are available to you! This is what Paul meant when he testified, "Not I, but Christ liveth in me" (Galatians 2:20). The Christian life is not lived by *imitation*, but by *incarnation*: He lives out His life in and through you!

Do you know by faith what it means to be "strengthened with might by his Spirit in the inner man" (Ephesians 3:16)? Do you draw upon Christ's limitless resources of grace by claiming His promises and calling upon Him in prayer? No matter what spiritual demands are made upon you, your Savior is sufficient to meet them. Christ can enable you to be an effective witness at work, a good husband and father at home, a winsome neighbor on your street. Don't depend on your own strength today. Depend on the sufficiency of Him who is all-sufficient for every spiritual need in your life.

Better Than a "Silver Lining"

During the early days of the Great Depression in the United States, people talked and sang about the clouds having "a silver lining." One skeptic said, "It's fine for a cloud to have a silver lining, but how do you get it to the mint so you can spend it?"

Jesus Christ is not only sufficient for a man's spiritual needs, but He is also sufficient for his *material* needs. Look at 2 Corinthians 9:8: "God is able to make all grace abound toward you; that ye, always having all sufficiency in all things, may abound to every good work."

All grace—*al*ways—*all* sufficiency—*all* things—*every* good work! Talk about a man-sized promise for Christian living today!

Certainly God is concerned about your material needs. He feeds the birds of the air and even takes note when a tiny sparrow falls dead to the earth. Second Corinthians 9 deals primarily with a special offering Paul was receiving to assist the poor saints in Jerusalem. Paul assured his readers that their faithful stewardship would result in God's faithful care of their needs. "Because you are faithful to give to others," Paul wrote, "your Lord will be faithful to care for you."

Of course, if a man is careless in his stewardship, he cannot honestly claim this promise. But the Christian who knows how to give to the work of the Lord will find God *giving back to him* in greater measure than ever he gave to others. Christ is sufficient for every material need that a believer faces when he is in the will of God.

Aches and Pains—and Prayer!

There's that wonderful word *sufficient* again! "My grace is sufficient for thee" (v. 9). Jesus Christ is able to meet our physical needs as well as our spiritual and material needs!

Perhaps you, too, have a "thorn in the flesh"—some physical affliction that God has permitted in your life. Paul's affliction was not the result of sin or careless living on his part; rather, it was given to him *to keep him from sinning*. Like his Lord in Gethsemane, Paul prayed three times that God would remove the thorn; but God did not do so. God did not answer Paul's prayer affirmatively, *but He did meet Paul's need!* He gave him the grace to turn pain into victory and weakness into power.

The older a man gets, the more he appreciates a strong, healthy body. Certainly a Christian ought to take good care of "the temple of the Holy Ghost" (1 Corinthians 6:19) for Jesus' sake and for the sake of those who depend on him. But the older we become, the more we feel the "burden of the body"! How easy it is to excuse ourselves from Christian responsibilities simply because we "don't feel up to it."

Christ purchased your body when He died for you on the cross. He wants you to glorify Him and magnify Him through your body (Philippians 1:20-21). He knows your physical weaknesses, and His grace is sufficient to overcome them. Only Christ can change weakness into strength! If today you just "don't feel up to it," read 2 Corinthians 11:23-33 and see what the grace of God did for Paul!

The Forgotten Giant

Everyone knows the story of David killing the giant Goliath (1 Samuel 17), but did you know that there was *another* giant in David's life—one whom David was not able to kill?

Ishbi-benob was the giant's name, and, like Goliath, he was a Philistine. David bravely faced the enemy, but the giant proved too much for the king! It took Abishai, David's nephew, to rescue the king from certain death.

Let's learn a few lessons from this story of the forgotten giant.

For one thing, *God does not always do the miraculous.* God directed David's sling and stone when he faced Goliath; but when it came to Ishbi-benob, God used Abishai's sword. Sometimes God does the unusual; more often, He uses the means available to get the job done.

Here's another thought: *giants have a way of coming back!* We never outgrow temptations and trials. Yes, as a young man David killed Goliath; but as an older man he faced one of Goliath's relatives! "Watch and pray" is sound spiritual counsel for every Christian, for you never know when there is another giant around the corner. "Let him that thinketh he standeth take heed lest he fall" (1 Corinthians 10:12).

You cannot always win the battle alone. Years before, David was the sole hero when Goliath was slain. But the next time he faced a giant, David needed help. His nephew Abishai had proved to be a headstrong and fiery youth, and David had not always agreed with what he did. But Abishai (with all his faults) was the man God used to save the king's life. It may surprise you when you arrive in heaven to discover the Christians here on earth that God has used to help you along the journey of life.

13

Praying with Your Eyes Open

"We made our prayer . . . and set a watch" (v. 9). This was the secret of Nehemiah's victory over the enemies that tried to hinder the rebuilding of the walls of Jerusalem. The New Testament in several places has picked up this secret and applied it to different areas of your Christian life.

"Watch and pray" is the secret of victory over *the world.* In Mark 13 our Lord describes the trying conditions that will exist in the world in the last days, conditions that could well draw a believer away from the Lord. "Take ye heed, watch and pray." He counsels in verse 33, "Pray with your eyes open and the world will not seduce you from loyalty to Christ."

"Watch and pray" is also the secret of victory over *the flesh.* When Jesus left Peter, James, and John in the Garden, He warned them, "Watch ye and pray, lest ye enter into temptation. The spirit truly is ready, but the flesh is weak" (Mark 14:38). Peter did *not* "pray with his eyes open," and he walked right into temptation and sin.

"Watch and pray" will also give victory over *the devil* according to Ephesians 6:18. In the preceding verses, Paul describes *the enemy* we face and *the equipment* we must wear; but he makes clear that *the energy* for spiritual victory comes from "watching and praying." Be alert and pray! Don't go to sleep while you pray!

Finally, "watch and pray" is the secret of finding open doors for our Christian witness and ministry. Read Colossians 4:2-4 and start praying with your eyes open!

14

Any Unpaid Debts?

No man likes to live under the burden of unpaid debts. Of course, an honest debt is often a stimulus to harder work and greater thrift! But most of us are happy when the debt is finally paid.

Christians have some *spiritual* debts that, in one sense, can never fully be paid. Romans 1:14-15 informs us that we are debtors to *every lost soul* to tell them the good news of the gospel. "I am debtor!" cried Paul. "I must carry the gospel to the last lost soul!"

Romans 8:12-13 indicates a second debt—our debt to the Holy Spirit. Paul makes clear that you have *no* debt to the flesh! Yet how prone we are to take care of the flesh and ignore the Spirit! Suppose the Holy Spirit had not convicted you of sin? Suppose He had not opened your eyes to the truths of the Word of God? Suppose He had not imparted saving faith to your heart? *You would still be lost!*

How do we pay our debt to the Holy Spirit? By keeping His temple clean; by obeying His leading and not grieving Him; by studying the Book that He wrote about Jesus Christ; by yielding our bodies to Him to be used to win others to Christ.

Any unpaid debts in your life?

You're Not Out of Debt Yet!

Consider two more spiritual debts.

What about your debt to *your weaker brethren?* All of Romans 14 deals with this problem. One Christian does this, another Christian condemns him and does something else. Some Christians are strong in their faith and enjoy the spiritual liberty in Christ, whereas other Christians are weak in faith and live in bondage to rules and regulations. What is a man to do?

Well, the Christian man has a debt to his weaker brethren to love them and never put a stumbling block in their way. "Owe no man any thing, but to love one another," Paul exhorts in Romans 13:8, and that's one debt we will never completely settle! If we live to please ourselves, then our lives will hurt our weaker brethren; but if, like Christ, we live to please others *for their own good*, then we will build them up.

In 15:25-27, Paul reminds us of our debt to *the Jewish nation*. Paul was at that time taking a relief offering to the Jews at Jerusalem, a token of the love and concern of the Gentile churches he had established. "Salvation is of the Jews." Gentile Christians in this present age have a spiritual obligation to the Jews, for apart from them there would be no Bible or no gospel. "Pray for the peace of Jerusalem: they shall prosper that love thee" (Psalm 122:6).

A Man Has to Eat!

That's right, a man *does* have to eat! But if he is going to be a *whole* man, he must feed the soul as well as the body. "Man shall not live by bread alone, but by every word that proceedeth out of the mouth of God." The outward man is perishing, yet needs to be fed; so how much more the "inner man" that will live eternally (2 Corinthians 4:16).

The average healthy adult male eats three good meals a day —and probably several snacks! Do you take time to feed on the spiritual nourishment in the Word of God? Job confessed that he valued the Word of God more than his necessary food. He would rather meditate on the Word of God than enjoy a steak dinner!

God's Word is food for the inner man, and it sets before you daily a well-balanced diet. There is the *milk of the Word* (that you never really outgrow) according to 1 Peter 2:2; and, for the mature saint, there is the *meat* of the Word, the deeper truths about Christ's present ministry as High Priest in heaven (Hebrews 5:6-14). Jesus compares the Word to *bread* in Matthew 4:4, and the psalmist writes, "How sweet are thy words unto my taste! Yea, sweeter than honey to my mouth!" (Psalm 119:103). Milk—meat—bread—honey! What a spiritual menu the Lord has set before us for the inner man!

Of course, merely *reading* your Bible will not nourish you, any more than reading a cookbook or a restaurant menu will feed a starving man. You must make the Word a part of your inner life by understanding it, meditating on it, memorizing it, and obeying it. Only then will you grow in the inner man and be strong because the Word is abiding in you (1 John 2:14).

How Much Is Your Bible Worth?

Don't misunderstand the question. It isn't, How much did your Bible cost? because that is not important. The question is, How much is your Bible worth? The way you value God's Word pretty well reveals the kind of a Christian you really are.

The psalmist valued God's Word above gold and silver—and even above the rich spoils of war. (By the way, there's a suggestion in Psalm 119:162 that we must battle before we can claim the spoils of God's Word. Bible study demands the courage and discipline of a soldier!) The psalmist would rather discover the treasures of God's Word than the treasures of kings.

It is really too bad that Achan did not have this same attitude. Unfortunately, he preferred *material* treasures to *spiritual* treasures. He decided to have the ungodly spoils of war instead of the holy words of the Lord. The result was disastrous, both for him and his nation.

Note in Joshua 8:2 that God permitted Israel to take the spoils from Ai. Had Achan valued God's Word above the spoils and waited another day, he would have enjoyed all the riches his tent could hold! Reminds you of Matthew 6:33, doesn't it?

It is in the everyday decisions of a man's life that he discovers the true values of his Christian life. The man who lies or cheats to make himself a success, instead of obeying the Word and trusting the Lord, clearly proves what his values are. He values money above God's Word.

How much is *your* Bible worth?

What Shall We Say?

Paul had been writing about the great things of the Christian life, including *suffering*. All of creation is suffering under the curse of sin, and even the most devoted Christian feels the burden of suffering in one way or another.

"What shall we then say to these things?" he asks in verse 31, and he himself gives us the answers.

"We know that *all things* work together for good" (emphasis added). There's an answer for you! The trials and demands of life are not working *against* us; they are working *for* us—and *God is in control*. The individual trials of life may perplex us, but He knows how to put them all together for our benefit. The separate ingredients that the pharmacist mixes into a prescription might harm us, but, when properly mixed, they bring health. God knows how to "mix" the ingredients of life, you can be sure.

"Shall he not . . . freely give us *all things*?" (v. 32, emphasis added). The logic of this statement is obvious: if God cared enough to give us His best, Jesus Christ, then surely He will give us whatever else we may need. God will not give us all that we want, but He will never withhold what we really need.

"In *all these things* we are more than conquerors through him" (v. 37, emphasis added). The problems and burdens of life will make you either a victor or a victim, depending on whether your faith is in yourself or in Christ. No enemy on earth or in hell can conquer the trusting saint. "If God be for us, who can be against us?" asks verse 31. We are not simply conquerors through Christ; we are *more than conquerors*.

The "things of life" will assault you day by day, but you need never fear, fret, or fail. In Christ you have the victory.

If?

Just as large doors swing upon small hinges, so great truths hang upon little words. The word *if*, used three times in this passage, carries with it some important truths for the Christian.

There is the *if* of holiness: "If I wash thee not, thou hast no part with me" (v. 8). The word *part* means "partnership, fellowship." When you were saved, you were washed all over (v. 10) and your sins forgiven. But as you walk through this life, your feet become dirty. If you want to maintain that close fellowship with Christ, you must come to Him for cleansing. Peter did not realize that his dirty feet were hindering his fellowship with the Lord. The promise to claim here is 1 John 1:9.

But there is also the *if* of humbleness: "If I then, your Lord and Master, have washed your feet; ye also ought to wash one another's feet" (v. 14). What a gracious act of humility it was when Jesus arose, laid aside His outward garments, and girded himself like a servant in a towel! Peter may have had this in mind when he wrote years later, "Be clothed with humility" (1 Peter 5:5). Pride is the source of much contention and trouble. It is only by being humble and following Christ's example (John 13:15) that we can enjoy the blessing of God. For "God resisteth the proud, but giveth grace unto the humble" (James 4:6).

Finally, there is the *if* of happiness: "If ye know these things, happy are ye if ye do them" (John 13:17). Christian joy is not found simply in knowing God's Word; we must *practice* it if we are to receive the blessing. Obedience always leads to joy; disobedience always leads to sorrow. Christ is our "Lord and Master [Teacher]" (v. 14). He teaches us the truth and then commands us to obey. Best of all, He *helps* us to obey through the power of His Spirit.

If! A little word that can lead to big blessings.

Never Alone

What sustained Moses during those difficult years as leader of the nation of Israel? It was not his Egyptian education or his own personal strength. In fact, more than once he almost broke under the load and tried to quit. No, Moses was sustained by a promise: "He will not fail thee, neither forsake thee" (Deuteronomy 31:8). It was the promise of the presence of the Lord.

When Moses died, Joshua took over the rule of the nation; and the Lord gave him the same sustaining promise. "As I was with Moses, so I will be with thee: I will not fail thee, nor forsake thee" (Joshua 1:5). Moses needed the promise for carrying his burdens, and Joshua needed the promise for fighting his battles. And the promise *worked!*

The older a man grows, the more burdens he must carry and the more battles he must fight. How difficult it is for us to be both Moses and Joshua in our places of responsibility! But we have the same promise that they trusted: "Let your conversation [behavior] be without covetousness; and be content with such things as ye have: for he hath said, I will never leave thee, nor forsake thee" (Hebrews 13:5). Our Lord's last words to His disciples were, "Lo, I am with you alway, even unto the end of the world [age]" (Matthew 28:20).

The Christian is never alone. No matter what burdens you must carry or what battles you must fight, your Savior is at your side to help you. Yield control to Him, and allow Him to accomplish His purpose in and through you.

21

Enjoy Being a Christian

It surprises many Christians to discover that the word *enjoy* is found in the Bible. As a friend commented to me one day, "Most Christians *endure* the Christian life; they don't really *enjoy* it." But how can you help but enjoy being a Christian when you realize how rich you are in Christ?

You have, for instance, the "riches of his goodness" (Romans 2:4). "For the Lord is good," sings the psalmist (100:5), and *He is*! The everyday provisions for your needs, the sunshine and rain, the power to work—all of these are evidences of the goodness of God. The trouble is that too many Christians forget the goodness of the Lord and take these blessings for granted.

And, there are "the riches of his grace" (Ephesians 1:7). God in His grace meets every spiritual need you may have. He is "the God of all grace" (1 Peter 5:10), and "he giveth more grace" (James 4:6). He promises in 2 Corinthians 12:9, "My grace is sufficient for thee." God in His mercy does not give you what you *do* deserve, but God in His grace gives you what you *don't* deserve!

But please do not forget "his riches in glory" (Philippians 4:19). While on earth, Jesus was the poorest of the poor. But glorified today in heaven, He is the richest of the rich! Do you need strength? Ephesians 3:16 promises this strength "according to the riches of his glory." Turn to your glorified Lord in heaven and, by faith, receive what you need.

God wants you to enjoy the "true riches" of heaven (Luke 16:11) and not the passing riches of this world. Enjoy them today!

What Is God Looking For?

"Seeking fruit." These words describe what the Lord Jesus is looking for in the lives of His people. How patiently He cares for the tree, hoping that the fruit will appear. But if it does not appear, He will not permit it to take up space! What a warning to us.

What kind of fruit does the Lord want to find? For one thing, He wants us to *win souls*. "That I might have some fruit among you" was the yearning of Paul's heart as he planned his trip to Rome (Romans 1:9-13). Soul-winning ought to be the burden of the believer's life, seeking to win others to the Lord. It is not enough merely to know the Lord, attend church, support the Lord's work, and seek to live a decent life. *We must share Christ with the lost!* "Ye shall be witnesses unto me!" He commands us in Acts 1:8.

There is also the *fruit of the Spirit* (Galatians 5:22-23), which means the life of Christ seen in our lives. These Christian qualities cannot be manufactured or imitated; they must be produced by the Spirit in a living way. Fruit demands life; machines can manufacture shoes, but they cannot produce living fruit. Fruit demands light and water, and as the Christian walks in the light and drinks deeply of the fountain of living water, he will bear fruit for God's glory.

Hebrews 13:15 mentions *the fruit of the lips*, "the sacrifice of praise." How the Lord loves to hear His people praise and thank Him, and what a wonderful testimony thanksgiving is to the lost! Our personal witnessing ought not to be a cut-and-dried artificial thing; rather, it must be a *living* witness, the fruit of our lips coming from a loving and grateful heart.

Has the Gardener found any fruit in your life today?

God Is Still Seeking

God is not only seeking fruit in the lives of His children, but He is also seeking *true worshipers*.

We commonly think of worship in terms of stained-glass windows, choirs, and an order of service, but Jesus said nothing about these things. To Him, the most important factor was the condition of the heart, not the location or the position of the body. Worship is that adoring attitude of reverence that is lost in the glory and wonder of what God is. It is not simply thanking God for what He has done; it is praising Him for who He is. It is Job confessing that he is vile and unable to speak to God (Job 40:1-5). It is John beholding Christ's beauty and glory and falling as dead at His feet (Revelation 1:9-17). Yes, and it is that little child taken up in His arms to receive His love and His blessing.

God is seeking *true* worshipers, believers who worship Him in spirit and truth. Worship can be counterfeited by the flesh, but it will not be *true* worship. Fellowship with God that demands only architecture to look at, great choirs to listen to, and incense to smell is far below the kind of worship that God seeks. Only the indwelling Holy Spirit can lead us into true worship.

It must be *in truth*. This means a clean heart, a heart resting upon the truths of the Word of God. God is not seeking *ignorant* worship! He wants our hearts and minds filled with the words and truths of His Word. The more we learn about God from His Word, the deeper our worship will be.

God is seeking worshipers because *worship ultimately leads to service*. It cannot be a selfish thing! The true worshiper must eventually say, as did Isaiah, "Here am I; send me" (Isaiah 6:8).

24

The Seeking Savior

The Father is seeking worshipers; the Spirit is seeking His fruit in our lives; and the Son is seeking *the lost*. This is why He came, and this is why He died.

Someone has to seek after sinners simply because they *are* lost! Andrew went to *find* his brother Simon (John 1:41); and some concerned soul-winner had to come to find you and me.

The Lord Jesus found lost sinners everywhere He went. He found them by the seashore, at the dinner table, in the synagogue—and even up a tree! Of course, the sinner does not *realize* he is lost, but that makes his plight even worse. "All we like sheep have gone astray" (Isaiah 53:6).

Are you walking with the Savior and seeking the lost? Do you have a sincere burden for souls? Witnessing and soul-winning are not activities that we turn on and off like a radio; they are burdens that control our lives every minute of the day. There are opportunities to witness for Christ presented to us daily. How many lost people we could lead to Christ if only we really cared!

Here is a suggestion: in your daily devotional time, ask the Lord to make you a soul-winner and to use you *that day* to speak to someone about Christ. Then, watch for His leading. It will amaze you as you watch the Lord go before you to prepare the way. And it will bless you as you seek the lost and bring them to Christ.

One of the best ways to "follow His steps" is to go with Him seeking the lost.

25

A Matter of Thrones

Two thrones were involved in Nehemiah's experience that day: the earthly throne of the king and the heavenly throne of the Lord. And before Nehemiah asked the aid of Artaxerxes, he looked to God for wisdom and strength. No wonder he knew the blessing of "the good hand of . . . God" upon his life!

Perhaps Nehemiah was claiming the promise of Proverbs 21:1: "The king's heart is in the hand of the Lord, as the rivers of water: he turneth it whithersoever he will." This much is certain: the man who receives a hearing at the throne of grace (Hebrews 4:16) never has to fear the man on any earthly throne.

It is wise to keep your thrones in order. Before you talk to men about God's work, talk to God about the men. Before you turn to men for the weak help they can give, turn to God for His abundant provision. Christians who are habitually at the throne of grace never have to beg before men.

Esther 4:2 informs us that no man dressed in sackcloth was permitted to enter the presence of an Oriental king. You dare not bring any unhappiness or any distress into the king's court! Furthermore, the king might reject you and cast you from his presence! Not so with our heavenly throne of grace. We may come *boldly*, at any time, with any burden, and our King-Priest will hear us and answer.

"Having therefore, brethren, boldness to enter into the holiest by the blood of Jesus. . . . Let us draw near" (Hebrews 10:19, 22).

His Wonderful Gifts

This high-priestly prayer of the Lord Jesus is full of spiritual meat for your soul! To think that the Holy Spirit would record this conversation between the Father and the Son! But note, among other things, the three gifts Christ has left with us.

First, He has given us eternal life (v. 2). This is *salvation*. Eternal life, of course, is a *Person*: "He that hath the Son hath life" (1 John 5:12). Eternal life is a *gift*: "For God so loved the world, that he gave his only begotten Son" (John 3:16). Note in John 17:1-2 that the Father gave the Son authority to give eternal life *to those whom the Father gave to the Son*. What a wonderful blessing it is to be in the family of God!

He's also given us God's Word (v. 14); this is for our *sanctification*. "Sanctify them through thy truth: thy word is truth" (v. 17). It is not enough to receive the gift of eternal life once and for all; we must *daily* receive His Word into our hearts for the strengthening and cleansing of the inner man. The Bible is God's gift to us; what a sin to neglect it!

Finally, He has given us God's glory (v. 22). Note the tense of the verb: "I *have given* them." Romans 8:30 says, "Whom he justified, them he also glorified"—past tense. We have already been glorified; the blessing just has not yet been revealed! In fact, all of creation is groaning as it waits for the moment God's children will reveal that glory (Romans 8:18-23).

These three gifts cover every aspect of our salvation—past, present, and future: salvation, sanctification, and glorification. What more do you want?

A God of the Valley

The Syrians, of course, were superstitious people who could not believe in an almighty God, Ruler of heaven and earth. Their gods were limited to hills or valleys, and they thought the God of Israel was as their gods. How wrong they were!

The Christian life is like Canaan of old: it has its hills and its valleys (Deuteronomy 11:10-11). Egypt was a flat land, a monotonous land, because Egypt pictures this sinful world, with its boredom and monotony. The Christian life knows its mountain peaks of blessing, to be sure; but where there are mountains, there must also be valleys. And our God is just as much God in the valleys as He is on the mountaintops!

He is certainly God when we go through "the valley of the shadow of death" (Psalm 23:4). Have you ever noticed in that Twenty-third Psalm how the pronoun changes from "he" to "thou" in verses 3-4? In verses 1-3, David is talking *about* the Lord; but in verse 4 (in the valley), he is talking *to* the Lord—for He is right there with him!

Psalm 84:6 tells us about the "valley of Baca [weeping]." How many times God's people are called to go through the valley of tears and heartache, but the Lord is there! In fact, instead of leaving behind a pool of tears, the trusting saint leaves a *well of blessing* to refresh some other pilgrim. Only the Lord can turn a valley into a mountaintop of blessing!

If God is leading you into a valley, fear not; He knows the way out.

When All Else Fails, Read the Instructions

It was late Christmas Eve, and I was trying to put together our son's toy garage. The situation was becoming more and more frustrating. My wife smiled and said, "When all else fails, read the instructions." They were words fitly spoken.

The fate of that toy garage was nothing compared to the fate of that ship carrying the apostle Paul. He warned the centurion in charge that trouble lay ahead, but the centurion ignored him and gave orders to set sail. You know the rest: the promised storm blew up, the ship and its cargo were lost, and (by the grace of God) Paul and his companions were saved.

That Roman centurion made every possible mistake:

1. *He became impatient* (vv. 7-9, 12). He did not want to remain in that uncomfortable harbor; he wanted to get on the move. Impatience is a mark of immaturity and unbelief (read Isaiah 26:18).

2. *He listened to "expert advice" instead of God's Word* (vv. 10-11). No matter what the "experts" may say, depend on the truth of God's Word.

3. *He took a vote* (v. 12). As usual, the majority voted to leave—and the majority was wrong! The majority, you will recall, kept Israel out of the Promised Land; and the majority voted to crucify Christ! Obey God's Word even if the whole world is against you.

4. *He walked by sight, not faith* (v. 13). The "south wind blew softly" and was the signal (to him) to start moving. Beware of the "golden opportunity" that seems to contradict God's instructions. South winds often become stormy winds.

The only sure way to pilot your boat is to obey the Word, *come what may*.

The Other Brother

The fact that there were *two* brothers in that family is not incidental; it is basic to the meaning of the parable. The younger brother, of course, represents the publicans and sinners who were willing to repent and follow Christ, whereas his elder brother is an illustration of the Pharisees who criticized Jesus and His converts.

These two brothers illustrate two kinds of sins: sins of the flesh and sins of the spirit. The younger brother got involved in "riotous living" as he yielded to the desires of the flesh. The elder brother kept his body and life clean, *but he was still a sinner!* As Paul expresses it in 2 Corinthians 7:1, "Let us cleanse ourselves from all filthiness of the flesh *and spirit.*" That faithful older son may not have been guilty of filthiness of the flesh (and we're thankful), but what about filthiness of the spirit?

Here is where the dedicated Christian needs to take warning, for in God's eyes the sins of the spirit are just as bad as the sins of the flesh; and, in some ways, perhaps they are worse. The Pharisees were morally clean, but they were so proud and critical that no one could stand them. The elder brother was faithful to obey his father's commands, but he failed to share his father's love. He was hateful; he had an unforgiving spirit; he was proud and self-satisfied; he demanded special attention and pouted when he did not get his way! He publicly announced his brother's sins instead of hiding them under a covering of love.

David prayed, "Create in me a clean heart, O God; and renew a right spirit within me" (Psalm 51:10). A clean heart and a right spirit—what more could a Christian desire?

Learning How to Pray ✝

One of the great prayer promises of the Bible is Matthew 7:7—"Ask, and it shall be given you; seek, and ye shall find; knock, and it shall be opened unto you." See how this promise is illustrated in our verses for the day.

The ruler of the synagogue came *asking*. His daughter was dead and only Christ could make her alive again. His prayer was specific; it came from a concerned heart; it was uttered in faith. True, there was a delay in getting the answer, but the answer did come. He asked; he received.

The sick woman in the crowd came *seeking*. Weak and discouraged after many years of seeking a curse, she picked her way through the crowd to reach Jesus. What humility she showed as she bent low at His feet to touch the hem of His garment! She was healed instantly. "Seek, and ye shall find."

The two blind men *knocked* at the door of the house in which Jesus was staying, and the door was opened for them. Suppose they had stopped outside the door? Suppose they had not knocked long enough? They knocked, the door was opened, and they received their sight.

This simple prayer promise has worked for others, and it can work for you.

What Are the Sacrifices?

These verses describe the privileged position of the New Testament believer in Christ. We are "a royal priesthood" (v. 9) and "an holy priesthood" (v. 5); it is our privilege to "offer up spiritual sacrifices, acceptable to God by Jesus Christ." What are these spiritual sacrifices?

Let's begin with Romans 12:1: "I beseech you therefore, brethren, by the mercies of God, that ye present your bodies a living sacrifice." Not a dead sacrifice, but a *living* sacrifice, yielded on the altar every minute of the day. Our bodies must be burnt offerings, wholly surrendered to Him for His glory. For the practical side of this surrender, read Romans 6.

Prayer is another spiritual sacrifice: "Let my prayer be set forth before thee as incense; and the lifting up of my hands as the evening sacrifice" (Psalm 141:2). Prayer is more than a child telling the Father his needs; it is the priest offering fragrant incense to the great High Priest. When we look upon prayer as a spiritual sacrifice, it makes us realize how far short we fall in our prayer life.

A third spiritual sacrifice is *a broken heart*: "The sacrifices of God are a broken spirit: a broken and a contrite heart, O God, thou wilt not despise" (Psalm 51:17). How God rejoices to see a broken and contrite heart! "To this man will I look," says the Lord, "even to him that is poor and of a contrite spirit, and trembleth at my word" (Isaiah 66:2).

Have you brought these sacrifices to the Lord?

Still More Sacrifices

God looks for the sacrifice of *praise*. How easy it is for us to complain! How difficult it is to praise the Lord and thank Him for His mercies. "O that men would praise the Lord for His goodness!" exclaimed the psalmist. Continual praise accompanies a continual walk with the Lord. When we acknowledge His blessings and thank Him for them, our words are sacrifices on the altar, accepted by our High Priest.

Paul looked upon the church's missionary offering as a sacrifice given not to him, but to the Lord. How careless we are with tithes and offerings. Money represents a part of our lives, the labor we have expended; it ought to be precious to us as we give part of it to the Lord. Many believers just "drop something in the offering plate," and their actions are not spiritual worship.

"Ye brought that which was torn, and the lame, and the sick; thus ye brought an offering: should I accept this of your hand?" the prophet Malachi asked the priests of his day (Malachi 1:13). Imagine the priests of God keeping the best for themselves and bringing the castaways and rejects to the Lord! Unfortunately, some of God's priests do this very thing today. Is it any wonder they miss God's best blessings?

Let's be faithful priests and bring the best to Him.

Exercise Counts

If a man wants to be healthy, he must watch his food and exercise—and keep both in their proper proportion. Too much food without sufficient exercise will make a man overweight and sluggish, and too much exercise without the proper diet will make him sick.

What is true of the outer man physically is true of the inner man spiritually: the inner man needs the proper food and exercise. In verse 6 Paul names the nourishing food—the "words of faith and of good doctrine." And he warns about the *wrong* diet —"profane and old wives' fables" (v. 7), that is, the empty doctrines and traditions of men, doctrines that cannot be supported by the Word of God.

But along with spiritual food there must be exercise. Paul is not saying that bodily exercise is not profitable, because every man knows that it is. Rather, he is arguing that physical exercise is profitable for only a little time, whereas spiritual exercise is profitable in this life *and* in the life to come. The balanced Christian will invest his time in both, but he must remember that spiritual exercise must take the priority.

To "exercise unto godliness" means to put into practice the rules and requirements for a godly life. Certainly it includes prayer and witnessing, meditation on God's Word, and the good works that the Spirit enables us to perform. It implies discipling the life, exercising the conscience (Acts 24:16), and using the "spiritual senses" God has given us (Hebrews 5:14).

Food and exercise—these are the ingredients for a healthy Christian life.

A Visit to Court

The prophet Zechariah ministered to the Jewish remnant that returned to Jerusalem after the Babylonian captivity. They were "a poor lot," and Satan did all he could to frustrate their plans. The vision the prophet saw revealed the sinfulness of the people; for, in God's sight, the high priest's garments were covered with filth. As Joshua the high priest stood before the Lord, he symbolized his wayward people.

Satan was also there. What was he doing? He was accusing the people before God and asking that a just God condemn them for their sins. As the accuser of the brethren, Satan accuses us before God night and day (Revelation 12:7-12).

But Christ is also there! If Satan is the accuser, then Christ is the Advocate, the heavenly Lawyer who represents us before the throne of God. "If any man sin, we have an advocate with the Father, Jesus Christ the righteous" states 1 John 2:1. He stands there, still bearing the wounds of the cross. It is because of Him and His shed blood that the sinning saint can claim the promise of forgiveness: "If we confess our sins, he is faithful and just to forgive us our sins, and to cleanse us from all unrighteousness" (1 John 1:9).

Listen to the accuser and you will become discouraged and quit. But turn to your Advocate in confession, and God will change your clothes! "Who is he that condemneth? It is Christ that died, yea rather, that is risen again, who is even at the right hand of God, who also maketh intercession for us" (Romans 8:34).

35

Doing the Washing

You know the story behind Psalm 51. David had fallen into horrible sin, even to the point of having an innocent man murdered. He tried to cover his sin for nearly a year, but then God found him, and David's heart broke with this prayer of confession. There is only one prayer a believer can pray when his sin is before him: "Wash me!"

But cleansing should not stop there. In Isaiah 1:16 the Lord says, "Wash *you*, make you clean" (emphasis added). In other words, it is up to us to put out of our lives the things that displease the Lord. "Let us *cleanse ourselves* from all filthiness of the flesh and spirit" (2 Corinthians 7:1, emphasis added). We must not expect the Lord to do this for us. If our hearts are truly repentant, we will put away sin from our lives.

There is yet a third step: *wash one another*. In John 13:12-17, Jesus teaches His disciples to wash one another's feet; that is, to show humility one to another and seek to help our fellow saints keep clean. In Acts 16:33 the newly saved jailer washes the apostles' wounds. What blessings would come to our homes and churches if only God's people would cleanse the wounds they have caused in the lives of others!

Wash me—wash yourself—wash one another. The one experience naturally leads to the other. It's just a matter of getting started.

The Importance of Hiding

There are two divine commandments here: "Go, hide thyself!" and "Go, show thyself!" The first was probably more difficult to obey because Elijah was a fiery prophet who wanted to deliver his message and bring his people back to God. Yet, God took him out of circulation for three-and-a-half years (James 5:17) until His time arrived for judgment.

Why did God "hide" Elijah? There may be many reasons, but certainly the most important is this: He was preparing the prophet for the great contest with Baal on Mount Carmel. During those three-and-a-half years of retirement, Elijah was learning to wait, to pray, and to trust God for every need. Also, he was learning the value of being a blessing to only one person. Before he could show himself, the prophet had to hide himself and learn the lessons God had prepared for him.

Too often today God's people *show* themselves before they are ready to serve, and then they have to go *hide* themselves in shame! We are so anxious to serve the Lord that we forget to worship. Yet, the success of a man's public ministry depends on the success of his private fellowship with God. It is fine to go "without the camp" to serve Him (Hebrews 13:13), but first we must go within "the veil" to worship Him (Hebrews 10:19-20).

If God puts you in hiding for a season, do not fret over it. He is preparing you for an even greater ministry in the days to come.

Our God Is Able!

What a dramatic story this is! And what a thrilling example of faith and courage. Christian men today may not face the ordeal of a fiery furnace, but they do face situations almost as demanding. How easy it is to "cut corners" or "cross your fingers" and forget that you belong to the Lord! The three Hebrew children could have found all kinds of excuses for obeying the king's command, but they preferred to obey the Word of God.

"Our God . . . is able" (v. 17). This has been the testimony of believing saints down through the years. *He is able to deliver.* God does not promise to *keep* us out of difficulties, but rather to *bring* us out. He permitted the three men to go into the furnace —and then *went in with them!* He shares every trial you experience and enables you to come out a stronger and a better man and, through it all, to glorify Him.

God is able to keep. "Unto him that is able to keep you from falling" (Jude 24). At the beginning of your Christian life, you probably asked yourself, *Am I able to remain true to the Lord? Do I have the strength to hold out?* Then you discovered that *He holds you!* He is able to keep you from falling, or as others translate it, *stumbling.* The good Shepherd cares for His sheep.

God is able to *provide all that you need.* Read 2 Corinthians 9:8 in your Bible, and mark it. And believe it!

Our God is able. No, let's make it personal: *MY* GOD IS ABLE!

Where There's Life There's Hope

Hope is one of the great words of the Christian faith. It is one word the unsaved man simply cannot use, for the unsaved do not have any hope (Ephesians 2:11-13). But the Christian has hope because he has life in Christ.

We have hope because of *salvation*. We have been justified by faith (which means we have a right standing before God through Christ), and we have access into the grace of God, and we "rejoice in hope." We have a joyful hope in Christ! This "hope" is not a vague dream, a "hope so" feeling; it is a divine certainty. In fact, Paul said that Jesus Christ *is* our hope (1 Timothy 1:1).

But we also have hope through *suffering*. He says, "Tribulation worketh patience; and patience, experience; and experience, hope" (Romans 5:3-4). Suffering makes the unsaved man give up all hope; but when a Christian suffers, he rejoices in hope because He knows that God is in control. The darker the night, the brighter gleam the stars of God's promises. Romans 8:17 informs us that to suffer with Christ means we shall also be glorified with Him!

The Christian also has hope because of the *Scriptures*: "That we through patience and comfort of the scriptures might have hope" (Romans 15:4). No book inspires hope and encouragement like the Bible. Whether you read of God's dealings with Abraham or His blessings on Paul, you find your hope becoming stronger. This is because the *Holy Spirit* uses the Word to increase your hope. As Paul prays in Romans 15:13, "That ye may abound in hope, through the power of the Holy Ghost."

Where there's life (salvation), suffering, the Scriptures, and the Spirit, there's hope!

39

Remember the Clay

"For he knoweth our frame," says Psalm 103:14; "he remembereth that we are dust." God remembers, but we often forget! We believe we are made of steel or of gold, but God knows we are made of dust.

Why? Well, for one thing, clay is a humble material that is worthless apart from the skillful hands of the potter. Clay is material with great potential; it can be molded into something useful. God has a purpose for every life, and the clay dare not argue about it. "Hath not the potter power over the clay?" asks Romans 9:21, and naturally the answer is, "Of course He does!"

It is when the clay fails to yield to the potter that the vessel becomes marred. *All clay can do is yield!* It cannot mold itself; it can only surrender to the potter and allow him to do the molding. But if the clay fails to yield, the vessel is marred.

But see the patience of God: "He made it again another vessel" (Jeremiah 18:4). If a life has been marred through sin and rebellion, there is always the forgiveness of God and the opportunity to start afresh. Abraham needed a second chance—so did Jonah and so did Peter. The Potter is willing to forgive and go to work again on the vessel, for He longs to make it "meet for the master's use" (2 Timothy 2:21).

The only time the Potter cannot remold the vessel is when the clay has become so hard that it no longer responds to His touch. Is it any wonder the Word warns us often against the hardening of the heart?

Full or Empty?

Did you notice the contrast between the two events recorded in our Scripture passage for the day? The multitudes came to
Christ hungry and empty, and they went away *full;* but the Pharisees came asking, and He sent them away *empty!*

These events illustrate the principle stated in Luke 1:53:
"He hath filled the hungry with good things; and the rich he
hath sent empty away." Had the Pharisees humbled themselves
and admitted their poverty, Christ would have helped them. But
they were too proud to bend, too proud to admit a need; and
they went away paupers.

God is partial to paupers. Not the lazy and the slothful, of
course, but those who know their spiritual needs and admit
them. "Blessed are the poor in spirit: for theirs is the kingdom of
heaven" (Matthew 5:3). "He raiseth up the poor out of the dust,
and lifteth up the beggar from the dunghill," Hannah sings in
1 Samuel 2:8. Christ would have blessed that church in Laodi-
cea, but the members did not know they had a need. "Thou
sayest, I am rich, and increased with goods, and have need of
nothing; and knowest not that thou art wretched, and miserable,
and poor, and blind, and naked" (Revelation 3:17).

Never be ashamed to confess your need to God. If you come
empty, you are sure to go away full if you allow Him to have His
way.

41

Taking Spiritual Inventory

Every factory and store has to close down for a short time to take inventory, otherwise the management will not know the true condition of the firm. Christians need to take inventory too, and in this chapter Hosea asks his people to examine themselves. He presents four pictures to help us.

1. *"A cake not turned"* (v. 8). This raises the questions, How deep is my spiritual life? Am I a "half-baked" Christian? Does the fire of the Word go deep into my life, or is my Christian life a shallow, surface thing?

2. *The "gray hairs"* (v. 9). Gray hairs are usually a sign of old age and declining powers. The people were becoming old and weak *and did not realize it!* Like Samson, they tried to use strength that they no longer possessed (Judges 16:19-21). How *strong* is my spiritual life? Am I pretending to be spiritually vigorous when sin has robbed me of my power?

3. *The "silly dove"* (v. 11). The prophet watched his people "flit" between Egypt and Assyria, first leaning on one, then on the other. How like some of God's people today: one day they walk with the Lord, and the next day they run to the world. "A double minded man is unstable in all his ways," says James 1:8. The silly dove that flits from one place to another soon finds himself without a refuge, and he is left alone. How *serious* is my devotion?

4. *The "deceitful bow"* (v. 16). Who wants to fight with a crooked weapon that cannot be trusted? This prompts the questions, *How dependable* is my Christian life? Can God depend on me? Can my church depend on me?

Here are four important questions about your Christian life: How deep is it? How strong? How serious? How dependable? The answers are important too!

The Boldness of the Believer

How bold would you and I be if we were summoned before the council to defend our faith? How Christian men need *boldness* in this day when so many Christians cringe before the enemy and fail to stand up for Christ! Where did this boldness come from?

It came from *being with Jesus* (v. 13). "Unlearned and ignorant" does not mean stupid or dumb; it means "not taught in the schools." Peter and John did not get their message or their power from some rabbi; they received it as they walked with Christ. The more we abide in Christ, the more He puts His strength in us and enables us to be bold in our witness.

Boldness also comes from *prayer* (v. 29). The apostles hastened back to their fellow Christians, and together they prayed for boldness. Note that it was not boldness to argue or to fight, but boldness to witness for the Lord in the face of ridicule and persecution.

Finally, boldness comes from *the Spirit's fullness* (v. 31). "The arm of flesh will fail you, ye dare not trust your own," warns the hymn writer. Only the Holy Spirit can take hold of your mind and heart and lips and make you a bold witness for Christ. How eager the Spirit is to use you as His witness! If you are grieving Him in any way, He will never fill you and use you; but if you are surrendered to Him, He will make you a courageous witness for Christ.

Take time to read Hebrews 4:14-16. You will discover that the Christian can have boldness on earth because he has *boldness in heaven* at the throne of grace!

Get On the Scale!

What a startling statement Hannah makes in verse 3: "For the Lord is a God of knowledge, and by him actions are weighed." You and I can weigh only material things, but God can weigh the spiritual. He sees whether our lives are made up of "gold, silver, precious stones, wood, hay, stubble" (1 Corinthians 3:12). Certainly He weighs the *motives* behind our actions. Jesus told the Pharisees that they lost their reward because they lived for the praise of men. He weighed their actions and revealed their hypocrisy.

God is able to weigh *the inner man.* "The soul of the diligent shall be made fat," promises Proverbs 13:4. This suggests that the inner man, the "hidden man of the heart" (1 Peter 3:4), grows in response to our spiritual diet and exercise. "He that putteth his trust in the Lord shall be made fat," says Proverbs 28:25. Faith adds spiritual muscles to the inner man and helps us grow in the Lord.

How sensitive many people are when you talk about their weight—or lack of it! Are we just as sensitive when it comes to weighing the inner man? Is God going to say to us, "Thou art weighed in the balances, and art found wanting" (Daniel 5:27)?

Let's Take Your Temperature

No matter what the ailment is, the doctor usually begins his examination by saying, "Let's take your temperature." The same principle applies to the Christian life, for there is more than one "spiritual temperature."

Some Christians are *cold*. "Because iniquity shall abound, the love of many shall wax cold" (Matthew 24:12). A cold Christian has no concern for lost souls. His prayer life is irregular, *if* he prays at all. He ignores his Bible and the fellowship of other Christians in the church. A cold-hearted Christian is a poor advertisement for Jesus Christ.

Other Christians are *lukewarm*. "I know thy works, that thou art neither cold nor hot . . . So then because thou art lukewarm. . . . I will spue thee out of my mouth" (Revelation 3:15-16). Lukewarm Christians, like lukewarm liquids, are made by mixing the hot and the cold. One day they are zealous for Christ; the next day they are living in the world. Lukewarm water is sickening. Lukewarm Christians make the Lord sick!

But, thank God, there are some Christians whose hearts are *burning!* "Did not our heart burn within us?" the Emmaus disciples asked each other (Luke 24:32). What caused their hearts to burn? They were walking with Jesus and listening to Him expound the Word! The fire of the Word (Jeremiah 5:14) can rekindle the flames on the altar of the heart.

Paul warned Timothy, "Stir up the gift of God, which is in thee" (2 Timothy 1:6). The image is that of stirring up a fire and adding fresh fuel, getting rid of the old ashes that smother the flame. Is your Christian life cold? Perhaps it is time to do something about the fire!

A Step at a Time

The patience of Jesus Christ is a wonder to behold. When He entered Peter's boat, He knew just what He would do. But He had to deal with Peter a step at a time, just as He must deal with us. Note Christ's commands to Peter.

Thrust out a little. Here Christ was asking for the fishing boat, and He converted it into a pulpit for preaching. It is likely that Peter sat in the boat with some impatience, wondering how long the sermon would last! Sometimes God moves us into trying situations just to get us to listen to His voice. Peter was a captive listener; he had nowhere else to go!

Launch out into the deep. This second command demanded more faith on Peter's part, and it's no wonder that he in essence argued, "We've been fishing all night! It's not likely we'll catch fish at this hour!" But the Lord knew what He was doing. Peter had given Him the boat; now Jesus wanted the fishing nets. And when Peter obeyed, God blessed them with a record catch!

Follow me! This was the supreme command, the one for which the first two were but preparation. Peter had thrust out a little and launched out into the deep; but now he had to "sell out" and give all to Christ. It was not enough to give Him the fishing boat and the fishing nets; Peter had to give Him the fisherman!

Jesus deals with us a step at a time, a command at a time, always leading to a supreme hour of faith and decision. If we obey Him in the little things of life, we will be ready when that "Follow me!" sounds in our souls. Let Jesus lead you and use you a step at a time.

46

Day and Night

These two passages seem to be contradicting each other. Jesus says that the night is coming, and Paul tells us the night is far spent.

Of course, there is no contradiction, because Jesus and Paul are talking about two different nights. Jesus is reminding us that we must work *today* while we have the opportunity, because the night is coming, and we will not be able to work. Satan is out spreading darkness because he is the prince of darkness. Judas went out "and it was night" (John 13:30).

Paul sees this present age as a time of darkness, but the darkness is passing as we get nearer to the return of Jesus Christ. We are children of the day, not of the night (1 Thessalonians 5:1-9); therefore, we had better wake up, clean up, and dress up for the battle! Jesus is coming again, and we don't want to be caught napping!

As far as Christian witness is concerned, the situation is getting darker. We must work for Christ while it is day; we must redeem the time—buy up the opportunity—before the darkness engulfs the world. But we must realize that although darkness is coming to the world, the light is about to dawn for the Christian. The day star is about to appear! "Now, little children, abide in him; that, when he shall appear, we may have confidence, and not be ashamed before him at his coming" (1 John 2:28).

47

Both Sides of the Coin

Bible doctrine is like a coin. It has two sides to it, and both sides are important. This present section on separation from sin is an example.

To begin with, there are two sides to sin: sins of the flesh and sins of the spirit. We have already illustrated this by the prodigal son and the elder brother (Luke 15). You and I may congratulate ourselves that we are "not as other men . . . extortioners, unjust, adulterers" (Luke 18:11); yet, we may be guilty of bad temper, impatience, anger or any of the other sins of the spirit.

And there are two sides to cleansing. We are to cleanse ourselves *and* to perfect holiness. One is negative, the other positive. One removes the stain; the other maintains the purity. It is not sufficient for the Christian to confess his sins; he must also forsake them and "take time to be holy." True repentance and confession ought to lead a man into a closer walk with Christ, a walk that will result in a holier and happier life.

There are also two motives for holy living: "having . . . these promises . . . in the fear of God" (2 Corinthians 7:1). The love of God and the fear of God! Are these two attitudes contradictory? Of course not! Just as a child loves and reverences his parents, so God's children love and fear Him. "Work out your own salvation with fear and trembling," commands Philippians 2:12. There are times when we obey Him because we love Him and enjoy His promises; and at other times our obedience will be motivated by a holy fear of God. Both are good. And both are necessary.

A New Point of View

A wise man has said, "It is more important to ask the right questions than to discover the right answers."

Peter asked a familiar question: "What are we going to get?" Christians today are *still* asking that question! Many church members, when asked to serve in an office of fill a responsible place of ministry, inwardly ask themselves, *What will I get out of this?*

That is the wrong question to ask. The Christian life is not a matter of *getting* so much as *giving*. I once saw a sign on a church bulletin board that read: "Christians are forgiven, forgiving, and *for* giving!" I agree!

Peter had made some giant steps in his spiritual walk when he moved from "What will I get?" to "Whatever I have, I'll give to you!" He was not interested in silver and gold once the power of the Spirit was at work in his life. He was more interested in touching other lives for Jesus Christ and seeing them transformed.

The most miserable people in the world are those who are always wanting to receive. The happiest people are those who live only to give to others. Of course, we have nothing of ourselves to give—our sufficiency is from Christ. We receive from Him and then share the blessings with others. We are channels of His wealth to a needy world of beggars.

Have you enriched anyone's life lately? No? Then why not start today?

Watch Out What You Worship!

The psalmist is using a bit of "holy sarcasm" as he describes the dead idols of the heathen, with their blind eyes and deaf ears. But in verse 8 he makes a startling statement: "They that make them are like unto them; so is *every one that trusteth in them."*

You become like the god that you worship!

Perhaps you have seen this in action in your own experience. You may know a businessman whose god is money. What kind of person is this businessman? Soft, tender, gentle, sensitive to the needs of others? Probably not. Rather, he is likely to be hard, insensitive, perhaps even brutal—*just like the metal he worships!*

The more we become involved with Jesus Christ, the more like Him we will be; and people will see the change in our lives. A man cannot spend time in the presence of Christ and not experience transformation. This is why we pray and read the Bible; this is why we fellowship with Him all day long in the everyday affairs of life.

Beware what you worship! You are becoming like your god —or your God.

Worship and Service

Never forget that Jesus Christ faced Satan and defeated him *as man* in a human body, depending on the power of the Spirit of God. In this way He shows us men how to face temptation and win the victory. Christ depended on God's Word—"It is written." Also, He had the Word ready in His heart and thus was able to silence the lies of Satan.

But it is a statement in verse 10 that interests us now: "Thou shalt worship the Lord thy God, and him only shalt thou serve." Satan had said nothing about *service;* all he wanted was *worship.* But Jesus knew that *whatever a man worships, he serves.* Let that saying sink down in your heart.

This is a surefire test for any man's life. Just find out what it is that takes up your time, energy, and money, and you will know what it is you really worship. What is the thing you sacrifice for? Then that is your god. Many men who would never think of being late for work ("I might get docked!") are never bothered by arriving late for church services. A headache would keep few men home from work, but it might excuse some from being faithful at God's house.

The thing you serve is the thing you worship. Are you truly worshiping God?

$$$$$$$$$$$

A college student, writing home to Dad, decided to "hint" that he was in need of more money. The letter began: "THING$ ARE $WELL ON CAMPU$. $OME OF THE $TUDENT$ ARE $IT-TING AROUND DOING NOTHING." The record does not show how Dad replied!

Riches—debts! Wages—taxes! Profits—losses! These are familiar words in a man's world. But wise (and wealthy) Solomon warns us that there are some things that money cannot buy, and one of them is a *good name*.

Money can buy popularity but not success. It can buy reputation—even fame—but not character. It can give you a living, but it can never buy life. "I'll give you a million dollars if you save my son's life," a man told the doctor in the emergency ward of a hospital. The doctor looked at the mangled body of the young man taken from a terrible accident, and said, "Mister, even if you gave me *ten* million dollars, I couldn't save his life!"

True riches, the kind that count both for time and eternity, come from the Lord. Humility and the fear of the Lord: these are the success factors in God's books. It is easy to live for the things money can buy and lose the things money *cannot* buy! The rich and poor will one day meet together before God. And, sad to say, some of those who are rich *now* will be poor *then*!

The Poor Rich Man

In this account, Jesus lets us look into the next world where everything is adjusted according to truth and reality. In *this* world, the rich man was rich, and the poor man was a beggar; but in *the next world,* the rich man became the beggar! What a switch!

Please do not misinterpret Christ's message. The rich man did not go to hell because he was rich, neither did the poor man go to heaven because he was poor. The rich man trusted his riches and lived for them; he left God out of his life. The beggar was poor in material things but rich in spiritual things. Verse 28 suggests that Lazarus had testified many times to the rich man, only to have his words rejected.

No, Jesus is simply emphasizing what He had already said in Luke 16:15—"That which is highly esteemed among men is abomination in the sight of God." What do most men value today? Money and power! Is God impressed with our wealth? The rich man used his wealth for himself and allowed the beggar to die on his doorstep. This in itself was evidence he did not know God.

How many poor rich men there are these days! And how many rich poor men! Which are you?

53

Let God Do the Work

Jonathan's statement in verse 6 ought to be the watchword of every believer today: "The Lord will work for us." God honored his faith and gave him victory, just as He will honor our faith today. Of course Jonathan did not sit down and expect God to do all the work alone. No, he made himself available as God's tool for the task that needed to be done.

God is working for you today, even in the difficult circumstances of life. Paul assures you that your "light affliction, which is but for a moment," is working *for* you and not against you (2 Corinthians 4:17). Suffering, heartache, burdens, disappointments —all of these actually work *for* the surrendered child of God who trusts God to work *for* him. Even tribulations work for us in developing Christian character (Romans 5:1-3).

Of course, Satan wants us to get our eyes off the Lord and on the circumstances of life, because then we will become so discouraged we will faint. "All these things are against me," Jacob complained when his sons brought him bad news from Egypt (Genesis 42:36); yet all things were actually working together *for his good*, because Joseph was down in Egypt getting ready to welcome his father and brothers into his heart and home!

"We know that all things work together for good to them that love God, to them who are the called according to his purpose" (Romans 8:28). "The Lord will work for us." Amen and amen!

Get in on the Secrets

There is a little parenthesis in verse 9 that shouts a message all its own: "But the servants which drew the water knew." They were in on the secret!

Someone has said that there are three kinds of men in the world: those who make things happen, those who watch things happen, and those who have no idea anything is happening. This is true in the spiritual realm. There are a few men who are being used of God to make things happen; there are many more who watch the others work; and there are multitudes who seem to be blind and deaf, unaware that God is even at work in this world!

The servants knew the secret. Those who know God's Word and obey it are always in on God's secrets. According to John 15:15, we are more than servants in the Lord's family; we are friends, confidants. He tells us His secrets!

But the key is *obedience.* "Ye are my friends, *if* ye do whatsoever I command you" (John 15:14, emphasis added). The servants in Cana obeyed His Word and learned His secret. And so may you and I.

Why Christians Cry

"I hate to see a grown man cry," a famous TV comic often says, and usually he gets a laugh. But the man is dead wrong. Sometimes the strongest thing a Christian man can do is to cry. After all, "Jesus wept." He was the Man of Sorrows.

In this psalm, David has been crying, and David was certainly no weakling! At the time he was fleeing from King Saul and had found a false refuge in Gath (read 1 Samuel 21:10-15). It seemed as though all the promises of God had failed. Instead of sitting on a throne as king, David was hiding in the wilderness like a wild animal.

Sometimes Christians weep, not because of their own sins, but because of the sins of others. David saw the nation going down into ruin because of the wickedness of King Saul. He knew that innocent people would suffer, and he wept. He saw men twisting his words and telling lies about him. Would this hiding and running and wandering ever end?

Well, it *did* end, and David inherited the throne! But his tears helped to make him what he was. He was a man after God's own heart (1 Samuel 13:14); for, after all, did not Jesus weep? Tears make us more like the Master, and that makes our tears worthwhile.

Again, Why Christians Cry

Christians also cry to *water the seed of the Word*. It takes tears of concern and compassion to see friends and loved ones come to Christ. It is not enough simply to sow the seed of the gospel; we must water that seed with our tears.

The "success formula" for winning souls is simple: going, weeping, sowing, reaping. No sowing without going, and no reaping without weeping.

Unconcerned Christians will never enjoy a harvest. It is the man who knows how to weep over souls who will see the seed take root and bear fruit. This was true of Paul's ministry in the difficult city of Ephesus. For three years he faithfully preached the Word, and Acts 19:10 states that "all they which dwelt in Asia heard the word of the Lord Jesus." Everyone had a chance to be saved! How did Paul accomplish that? Listen to his testimony in Acts 20:31: "Therefore watch, and remember, that by the space of three years I ceased not to warn every one night and day with tears."

A burden for souls is a sensitive thing; it is easily lost. And the test of that burden is whether or not we can still weep over lost souls. Dry eyes are often evidence of a hard heart, and a hard-hearted man does not win souls to Christ.

Genesis 50:22-26
Exodus 13:19
Joshua 24:32

Blessed Bones!

It is amazing that Joseph had any faith at all!

For one thing, he had been mistreated by his own family; and for some dozen years he had been forced to serve as a slave in Egypt. People had lied about him, and it appeared that his God-given dreams of reigning as a king would never be fulfilled. It would have been easy for this young man to follow the ways of Egypt and turn his back on his father's faith.

But he did not turn away! Instead, his trials only made him trust God even more. And when his time came to die, Joseph made his brethren promise to take his bones with them when God delivered them out of Egypt. He believed God's promises and wanted to share in the blessing of the deliverance!

Egypt, of course, is a picture of the world system that is opposed to God. "I don't belong in this wicked land of Egypt," Joseph essentially said. "I want to be buried in *our* land, in Canaan." That sounds like Paul: "For our citizenship is in heaven" (Philippians 3:20, NASB*).

Joseph knew what he believed, and he knew where he belonged. Oh, that we had more men like him today!

New American Standard Bible.

Enjoying God's Bonuses

Most men appreciate getting a bonus. It is a very practical way for an employer to say, "Thanks for a job well done!" It not only helps a man's wallet but also his ego. It's an extra boost no matter how you look at it.

God enjoys giving spiritual bonuses. He gave some to young King Solomon. God offered the new king anything he desired, and Solomon asked for spiritual wisdom and an understanding heart. How this pleased the Lord! So, the Lord not only gave Solomon his requests, but He added riches, honor, and victory as bonuses!

Why was God able to do this? Because if Solomon had the right values, and if he maintained the right kind of a heart, then God could *trust him* with these extra blessings. "By humility and the fear of the Lord are riches, and honour, and life" (Proverbs 22:4).

Jesus expressed it like this: "But seek ye first the kingdom of God, and his righteousness; and all these things shall be added unto you" (Matthew 6:33). Has God given you any bonuses lately? Perhaps you need to take inventory of your heart to see if your values are all they ought to be.

Let's Capture a Mountain

Age ought never to be a barrier to Christian service or victory. Here was Caleb, eighty-five years old, asking permission to clean out a nest of giants so he might claim a mountain for his inheritance. What a man of faith!

Most other men would have settled for a smaller inheritance—one that was less demanding. But not Caleb! "Give me this mountain" (v. 12). He had seen the Lord do great things in Egypt and in the wilderness, and he knew that God could do great things for him. "This is the victory that overcometh the world, even our faith" (1 John 5:4).

Caleb was a man of faith. He knew that God was true and that He kept His promises; so Caleb leaned heavily on the promises of God. He did not trust his own feelings or what men said about God's promises. He trusted the Lord.

All of us face mountains in our lives, those dangerous and seemingly insurmountable difficulties that lie before us. We can settle for a safe little retreat in the valley, or we can step out by faith and capture the mountain for the Lord. God is looking for overcomers like Caleb, men of faith who forget the difficulties as they boldly face the challenges. "Be of good cheer," said our Savior, "I have overcome the world" (John 16:33).

Get up, and capture that mountain!

Let's Get Stirred Up!

What a prayer this is! And what blessings we would know in our lives and churches if only we would pray like this and expect God to answer!

Whether you like it or not, *Isaiah was stirred up.* He wanted to see God do in his life and in his day what He had done in days gone by. "I'm not satisfied to *read* about God's miracles. I want to *see* them! I want to *share* them!"

Beware of the person who wants to rob you of a miracle-working God, who assures you that the power of God in answer to prayer can never be seen in this present age. Paul seemed to think that Isaiah was on the right track, because Paul quotes verse 4 in 1 Corinthians 2:9. "You have never really seen all that God wants to do for His people!" is what both Paul and Isaiah are in essence saying. How we need to hear them.

This raises a question: If God is still the same, and His promises do not fail, then why is it we are not seeing His mighty hand at work? Verses 5-8 answer the question: God's people are not in a position to receive His wonders. There is uncleanness, unconcern, unyieldedness. The fault is not with God; it is with us.

God is looking for a man who will become spiritually stirred, who will cry out to God for miracles, and who will pay the price to have his prayers answered. Will you be that man?

Romans 8:32
Ephesians 1:1-10
Philippians 4:13

A Matter of Prepositions

If you compare Ephesians 1:10 with Romans 8:32 and Philippians 4:13, you will find that "all things" is the theme of all three verses. But in each case there is a change in prepositions.

We have all things *in* Christ according to Ephesians 1:10. The third verse of that wonderful chapter makes clear that God has given you "all spiritual blessings" right now *in* Christ Jesus. You are rich *in* Him! Everything you need is already yours in Christ!

In Romans 8:32 Paul tells us that God enjoys giving us all things *with* Jesus Christ. His argument is this: If God gave us His very best when He sent His Son, then surely He will not withhold anything else that is good for us. But note that God gives us what we need *with* Christ Jesus. If the blessings cannot come with Christ, then they are not good for us.

Finally, you can do all things *through* Christ (Philippians 4:13). God does not depend on your power; He depends on Christ's power working in and through you. When you are weak, then He is strong.

Major on Jesus Christ. Make Him the preeminent One in your life. For you have all things *in* Him, *with* Him, and *through* Him—and nothing is greater than that.

No More! No More!

Recall for a moment the parable of the prodigal son (Luke 15:11-24). When the boy finally "came to himself" (v. 17), he got up and went home to confess his sins to his father. Remember his speech: "I . . . am no more worthy to be called thy son: make me as one of thy hired servants" (vv. 18-19). *No more worthy!* How often a sinning saint has felt that way!

But your Father does not want you to feel that way. No matter how greatly you may have sinned, your Father will forgive you and cleanse you. It is not a matter of your worthiness, for no one is worthy in God's sight. No, it is a matter of Christ's worthiness, the One who died for you!

Because of His death and resurrection, there is *"no more conscience of sins"* (Hebrews 10:2, emphasis added). Sacrifices can never wash away sins and make the inner man clean, but the blood of Christ can. And there is *no more remembrance of sins.* "Their sins and their iniquities will I remember no more" (v. 17). What a promise! Satan, the accuser, loves to remind us of our sins, but Christ the Savior has forgotten them—and He wants us to forget them too.

No more sacrifice for sins (v. 18)—this is the basis for it all! By one offering Jesus Christ settled the sin problem forever! "The blood of Jesus Christ his Son cleanseth us from all sin" (1 John 1:7).

Move from the "no more" confession of Luke 15 into the "no more" assurances of Hebrews 10.

What Happens When You Go to Church?

Church attendance is not a substitute for a daily walk with the Lord, but it is still an important part of the Christian life. Christians belong to each other and need each other. You find strength and encouragement in the fellowship of God's people.

What happened to Isaiah when he went into the Temple? For one thing, *he saw the Lord*. He looked beyond the other people in the building and saw God on His throne. Of course, we do not have such dazzling visions today, but we can still see the Lord as we meet with God's people. The Word of God, the worship, the praying, the fellowship—all of these can lift our eyes from this world with its problems and focus them on the King in heaven.

Then *Isaiah saw himself*. This is what usually happens when we see the Lord, for His glory and purity only reveal our shame and sin. "Woe is me!" cried the young prophet (v. 5). "What a sinner I am!" How easy it is to be convicted about *other people's* sins and never see our own shortcomings!

But the experience did not stop there, for *Isaiah saw the need*. He saw a world lost in sins and needing the message of the Lord. He went into the Temple a sinner and came out a soul-winner! God interrupted the "worship service" to send His angels down to make a witness out of Isaiah! For, after all, any experience with the Lord (if it is real) will make better witnesses out of us.

Is this what happens to you when you go to God's house?

It Takes Both

Proverbs 3:5-6 are familiar verses to Bible students, and they are important verses to those who really want God's best for their lives. They tell us that we must *believe God* and *acknowledge Him* if we want Him to direct our paths. Or to put it another way, we must "trust and obey."

After all, true faith always leads to obedience. "By faith Abraham, when he was called to go out . . . obeyed" (Hebrews 11:8). Bible faith is not a "good feeling" down inside, an emotion that we work up in our better moments. No, it is simply *confident obedience,* stepping out in obedience to God, knowing that He will keep His Word.

Jesus links these two as He talks about prayer. First, it takes *faith* to pray: "Whatsoever ye shall ask in my name that will I do" (John 14:13). But it also takes *obedience*: "If ye love me, keep my commandments" (v. 15). Trust and obey!

Interestingly enough, the more we obey Him, the easier it is to trust Him. But if we *say* we trust Him, but fail to obey, then even what little faith we do have seems to become dead and lifeless. Faith without works—obedience—is dead.

It takes both—faith and works, trust and obedience. This is the secret of guidance and the secret of answered prayer.

How to Keep From Backsliding

In verse 1 we meet "trust and obey" again! "I have walked in mine integrity" (that's obedience); "I have trusted also in the Lord" (that's faith). And what is the happy result? "Therefore I shall not slide."

When a Christian gradually gets away from the Lord, and sin comes into his life, this condition is called *backsliding*. It is not "*dropping* back," because it does not happen suddenly. It is a gradual thing, a sliding back instead of a moving forward in the things of the Lord. And when it happens, you may point to one of two causes: disobedience or lack of faith. And one leads to the other.

Faith in the Lord and faithfulness to the Lord will always keep the saint from backsliding. "My foot standeth in an *even* place," David announces in verse 12 (emphasis added). You cannot slide back on level ground!

As you read this psalm, note how David opens up his entire being to the Lord: "my reins," "my heart," "mine eyes," "mine hands," "my soul," "my life," "my foot" (vv. 2-3, 6, 9, 12). This wonderful openness with the Lord is essential to a faithful walk. Examine me! Prove me! Search me!

Too many Christians are living on a religious roller coaster —up one day, down the next. The secret of a level walk is "trust and obey." This is God's sure protection against backsliding.

Better Sober Up!

When Peter talks about being sober, as he does three times in his first epistle, he is not referring to sobriety as opposed to drunkenness. The word *sober* carries with it the idea of being serious and alert, taking life seriously and making the most of every situation. He gives us three great motives for living sober, serious lives.

First, *Christ is coming* (1:13). That means life will end—no more opportunities to win souls to Christ or to seek to build up His church. And it also means standing before His judgment seat and giving an account of our lives. What a serious moment that will be! The Christian who lives in the light of Christ's return is not going to waste time or money, neither is he going to waste opportunities to serve the Lord.

A second motive is in 4:7—*everything is coming to an end.* Be serious! Keep your eyes open! Pray! Why live for the things that will burn up? Why get wrapped up in the fleeting fashions of this world? Be sober!

Finally, *Satan is after you* (5:8)! No one laughs at a roaring, hungry lion! Jesting Christians would lose their smiles if they could see how Satan is ready to devour them. Life is not a playground; it's a battleground. It is time for Christians to be sober.

Certainly God's people have joy, but it is not the shallow, careless gaiety of the world. It is a deep joy that has a serious note, a watchful eye, a ready heart. A serious saint rejoices in the Lord and is ready to meet Him.

The Man at the Door

You are probably familiar with Revelation 3:20, where Jesus stands at the door and asks to be invited in. But did you know that your Savior still comes to the door seeking fellowship with His own?

Can you see yourself in this passage from Song of Solomon? The bride has retired for the night and is comfortable in her bed. But in her semiawake condition, she hears the voice of her beloved at her door. What does she do? She refuses to get up and let Him in. It is too inconvenient and, besides, she is already comfortably settled for the night!

What happens? The Lord leaves her door and disappears into the night! He leaves some perfume behind, but what is perfume compared to His wonderful presence in the house? The bride calls for Him, but He does not answer. It is as though He is saying, "I called to you, and you would not come. Now, when you call for Me, I will not come." It is the response of wounded love.

Christ comes to your door many times during the day. He wants you to pause for a moment, open the door to Him, fellowship with Him, and let Him enjoy your love. Does this sound mystical? It is the most *practical* thing in the world! After all, our children show us their most satisfying love, not when we command them to love us, but when they spontaneously jump into our laps and give us hugs and kisses. Every husband and wife knows that the spontaneous expressions of love mean more than the "routine" affections.

Take a "blessing break" during your day. It will mean much to you—and to your Savior.

Stung by the Honey!

Samson did not get stung by the bees; he was stung by the *honey*!

He was a Nazarite, which means he was never to drink strong drink, cut his hair (it was a mark of his dedication), or touch a dead body. When that lion attacked Samson, he was able to overcome it; but he was not able to overcome his taste for honey.

The moment Samson touched that honey, he was defiled. He lost his dedication and ceased to be a Nazarite. It was the beginning of the end.

Many times we face Satan when he comes roaring at us like a lion, and we are able, by God's grace, to overcome him. "Be sober, be vigilant; because your adversary the devil, as a roaring lion, walketh about, seeking whom he may devour," warned Peter (1 Peter 5:8). But after you have defeated the lion, *watch out for the honey!* Often Satan hides some "sweetness" in a dirty place, and we fall for his trap.

"How sweet are thy words unto my taste! Yea, sweeter than honey to my mouth!" So wrote the psalmist in Psalm 119:103. That was the decision Samson had to make: the sweetness of obeying God's Word, or the sweetness of the enemy's honey? And that is the decision *you* must make. Samson made the wrong decision. Will you?

The Turning Point

This long chapter deals with a deep problem, one that has perplexed God's children for centuries: Why do our unsaved friends seem to escape trouble while we Christians have more burdens than we seem to be able to bear?

In the first fifteen verses, the believer looks around and sees the apparent prosperity of his heathen neighbors. They are rich; he is poor. They escape sicknesses and sorrows; he is plagued by them. "I have become a Christian in vain!" he in effect cries. "Is it really worth it all to be saved?"

The turning point is verse 17—"Until I went into the sanctuary of God; then understood I their end." When he took the "inside view" of faith, then he saw the truth. He realized that the unsaved are really in slippery places and that their destiny is terrible to consider.

Read verses 23-28 whenever you feel that it is not worth it to be a Christian. God is with you; He holds your hand; He guides you in this life and promises to glorify you in the next life! The unsaved may have their passing riches, but we have the eternal God!

Whenever a Christian complains about his lot in life, it is usually because he is walking by sight and not by faith. He sees this world through human eyes and not through the eyes of God —the eyes of faith. The turning point from sighing to singing is *seeing* things the way God sees them; and you do this "in the sanctuary"—in the place of prayer and fellowship.

The Hidden Places

The prophet was permitted to see the inner life of the people back in Jerusalem. The Temple services were going along as usual, and everything seemed right on the outside; but on the inside—well, that was a different matter.

God showed Ezekiel what was going on for "every man in the chambers of his imagery" (v. 12). The people had adopted the gods of their heathen enemies and were worshiping them secretly in their hearts.

Man looks on the outside, but God looks on the heart. God is not impressed with our public worship; He sees what is going on in our hearts. How easy it is to pray with the lips while the heart is far from Him. And how easy it is for a man to have idolatry in his heart and evil images in his mind!

The Christian's body is God's temple (1 Corinthians 6:19-20). To have wicked imaginations is to defile the temple and grieve the Spirit of God. No wonder Ezekiel saw the glory of God depart from the Temple! And just as certainly God's glory will depart from our lives if we are unclean in the imaginations of our hearts.

Every man's prayer ought to be that of David in Psalm 19:14. Look it up, read it, and take it to heart.

A New Beginning

Don't criticize Peter for sitting in the boat and working on his nets. You can't help but admire a man who will work all night (fishing was his *job*, not his hobby) in spite of discouragement and who will work in the day to get ready to go back to work at night! Peter was no loafer. In fact, whenever God calls a man, He calls one who is *working*.

That is a good lesson to learn today: do the task that is at hand. Do it well, and do it diligently, and the Lord will lead you into greater things for His glory.

It did Peter a lot of good to sit in that boat (he was a captive audience) and to listen to Christ teach. After all, faith comes by hearing God's Word (Romans 10:17), and Peter would need real faith to obey the Lord and let down his net. When our Lord permits delays and disappointments in our lives, it is only that He might bring even greater blessings. Peter caught more fish in one trip than he ever dreamed he could do!

Best of all, *Peter saw himself.* The blessings God's Son brought to his life didn't make him proud and independent; rather, they made him humble and submissive. And the Lord promoted him! He became a fisher of men instead of a fisher of fish!

Yes, in the everyday activities of life—even in your job —Christ wants to come to bless you and to lead you into greater things. Will you let Him?

Childlike or Childish?

There is a vast difference between the Christian who is *childlike* and the one who is *childish*. Christ wants us to be like children in our submission, our love, our ignorance of evil (1 Corinthians 14:20), and our enthusiastic enjoyment of the blessings of life. But He does not want us to be *childish* in our disposition and attitude.

"When I became a man, I put away childish things," says Paul in 1 Corinthians 13:11. Nothing is more disgusting than an adult acting like a baby—pouting, fussing to have his own way, insisting on attention. The mature Christian who is growing in grace puts away childish things, the foolish "toys" that mark an arrested growth.

The Christian who lives for the flesh—the carnal Christian —will never mature and become a man of God. It is only through the Word and the Spirit that "babes in Christ" grow up to be "men of God." No wonder Paul wrote to the Corinthian believers, "Quit you like men, be strong" (1 Corinthians 16:13). In other words, "Stop acting like little kids! Grow up!"

It is expected that children will act childish; it is expected that men will act like men. Which are you?

Get the Right Wisdom!

Wisdom is the right use of knowledge for the glory of the Lord. But there are two sources of wisdom: from above (God's wisdom) and from below (the world's wisdom). It is important that you know the difference.

The wisdom of this world leads to envy, strife, confusion, and sin. Wherever people follow this wisdom, there is trouble. It is earthly (the world), sensual (the flesh), and evil (the devil) —and these are the three great enemies of the Christian.

But God's wisdom, which comes from above, always brings peace and joy. Instead of leading to fights, it leads to the peaceable fruits of righteousness. The Christian who lives by God's wisdom is a peacemaker, not a peace-breaker.

But this is not "peace at any price." In verse 17 James makes clear that God's wisdom is *first* pure, then peaceable. God always deals with *sin* before He gives peace. The reason men have never enjoyed lasting peace is because men will not deal with sin. "Peace at any price!" is their slogan. "Whitewash all that disobedience!" This is not wisdom; it is the height of folly.

Before there can be peace in your life, your home, your job, and your church, there must be purity; and this purity comes when you submit to the wisdom of the Lord, the Word of God. "The work of righteousness shall be peace; and the effect of righteousness quietness and assurance for ever" (Isaiah 32:17).

God's Success Story

A steward, of course, is a man who manages somebody else's property and is supposed to show a profit. All of us are stewards. We *own* nothing of ourselves; we only *possess* that which God has given us by His grace. Our job is to use His wealth for His glory.

Two of these men were successful, and they each received the same "bonus" from the master. What was their secret of success? *They were faithful with what they had.* The man with the two talents (a great amount of money) didn't complain because the other fellow had more; he went ahead and used what he had —and he received the same reward!

God gives us opportunities to match our abilities. Why did one man receive five talents? Because he had more ability, and even *that* was given him by the Lord. Success is not having a great deal of ability. No, success is using every opportunity to apply our abilities faithfully. If we can do more work, win more souls, invest more time, and we fail to do it, we are failing in the sight of God.

Rewards are based on the *proportion*, not the *portion*. The five-talent man made a 100 percent gain, but so did the two-talent man! Had the third worker gained only *one* more talent, he would have received the very same bonus!

Instead of complaining about the few abilities or opportunities you may have, begin using what you have faithfully—and see what God will do!

A Saved Mouth

The picture Paul paints of the mouth of the unsaved man is not a pretty one. He sees it as an open grave, full of poison and cursing and bitterness. Of course, the mouth is but the outlet for the heart, and the unsaved man's heart is just as full of sin and rebellion. The lost sinner cannot argue with God; every mouth must be stopped when God declares His judgment.

But what a change takes place when a man gives his heart to Christ! He believes with his heart, and then he confesses with his mouth. Because his heart has been cleansed, his mouth is clean too! The mouth that once was filled with cursing is filled with blessing; the bitterness is replaced by sweetness, and everything is new.

Then his mouth joins with others to praise God and bring Him glory! The Bible nowhere encourages "solo lives" but everywhere encourages us to join our hearts and mouths with those of other believers to glorify God. And just think of the great chorus we will join in heaven when Jesus returns!

A saved heart must lead to a sanctified mouth—a mouth that glorifies God. Is your mouth filled with the glory of God —or the poison of sin?

The Forward Look

Why are the laborers so few? There may be many reasons, but one of the main reasons is given in Luke 9:62—too many people *look back*.

Imagine how difficult it would be to plow while looking back! Plowing is not easy work; a man has to set his eyes on a fixed point and maintain that straight, steady line. Looking back is asking for a crooked line and a ruined field.

Why do Christians start serving the Lord and then look back? Two little words give the answer: "Me first." Two progressive disciples said, "Let me first . . ." If a man is going to work in the fields, he has to put himself last and the Lord of the harvest first. If each laborer tries to have his own way, the fields will never be prepared for the harvest.

"Let thine eyes look right on," commands Proverbs 4:25. "Remember Lot's wife," warns Jesus in Luke 17:32. She looked back and was judged instantly. "Forgetting those things which are behind," was Paul's testimony (Philippians 3:13). This is the forward look of faith that leads to victory and vitality in the Christian life.

In fact, this is the way our Savior lived while here on earth. Check Hebrews 12:1-2 and Luke 9:51-53. Imagine! These disciples were looking back while the Lord was looking ahead to the cross!

How to Get Bigger

This prayer was probably written when David was forced to leave Jerusalem during the rebellion led by his son Absalom. It was the most difficult period of David's career, and it appeared that everything was falling to pieces.

But see what these trials *did* for David: "Thou hast enlarged me when I was in distress" (v. 1). Instead of measuring his troubles, David was measuring *himself* to see if he were growing spiritually!

This, after all, is one reason God permits trials: they help us grow. Of course, if we rebel against God's will, troubles will break us down, but if we submit to His will, they will build us up. "The troubles of my heart are enlarged," David cries in Psalm 25:17. But God was using those troubles *to enlarge David!*

Paul was able to say with confidence, "We know that all things work together for good to them that love God" (Romans 8:28). "For our light affliction, which is but for a moment, worketh *for us*" (2 Corinthians 4:17, emphasis added).

Instead of resenting trials today, surrender to the Lord, and allow His grace to enlarge you spiritually.

Giants Wanted

Here is another of David's songs of trial and triumph; and once again the Lord brings blessing out of battles. Instead of being hemmed in by his troubles, David stepped out into "a large place" (v. 19).

This is the victory of faith, turning confining trials into enlarging experiences. They put Paul into prison, but God made it a "large place" as His servant ministered the Word of God. John was exiled to the tiny Isle of Patmos, but God opened the heavens to him and made the island a "large place" of blessing.

In verse 36 David says, "Thou hast enlarged my steps." He was able to take giant steps of faith because he had seen God at work in difficult circumstances. An enlarged heart (Psalm 4:1), a large place, and enlarged steps—what more could the believer want?

We are prone to complain about difficulties. How we need to remind ourselves that God-ordained trials are sent to accomplish God-ordained purposes. God presses us with trials that He might enlarge us! He enlarges our difficulties that they, in turn, may enlarge us and equip us for a larger place of service! No wonder Jabez prayed, "Oh that thou wouldest bless me indeed, and enlarge my coast" (1 Chronicles 4:10).

Let your trials make you a giant, not a midget.

No Place for Laziness

Twice in this passage Peter tells us to "be diligent"!

Be diligent to be sure you are saved (v. 10). Satan is the imitator, and he has many sincerely religious people believing they are saved and going to heaven. Can a person *know* that he is really saved? Of course! "Make your calling and election sure," said Peter (2 Peter 1:10). "Don't be satisfied with mere head knowledge or with emotional experiences. Rest your confidence on the finished work of Christ and the unchanging promises of God's Word."

In 1 Peter 1:4, Peter informs us that the true Christian shares God's very nature, and he proves that he has this new nature by turning away from the corruption in the world. "For whatsoever is born of God overcometh the world" (1 John 5:4).

But salvation is only the beginning. Peter continues by saying to be diligent to grow in your Christian life (1 Peter 1:5). Faith is the beginning, but there must follow virtue, knowledge, self-control, and the other wonderful fruits of the Christian life. Where there is life, there must be growth. "Desire the sincere milk of the word, that ye may grow thereby," Peter writes in 1 Peter 2:2. It takes diligence to grow; there is no place for laziness in the vibrant Christian life.

Be diligent! "Awake thou that sleepest" (Ephesians 5:14). Put as much effort and concern into your *spiritual* life as you put in your job, your home, your hobby. Be diligent!

How to Use a Sword

The Word of God is the "sword of the Spirit." Hebrews 4:12 tells us that God's Word is sharper than even a two-edged sword. But instead of piercing the body, it pierces even soul and spirit. The Spirit of God uses the Word of God to accomplish the will of God.

Nehemiah learned that it was not enough to have the sword alone; his men also needed *their tools*. You can battle with a sword, but you cannot build with it! Some Christians are so busy battling that they never build anything, and some build so carelessly they get caught by the enemy and lose what they have done for the Lord. As you wield the sword, be sure to work with the trowel and help to build the temple of the Lord.

Paul suggests that the sword needs to be associated with *prayer* as well. Praying in the Spirit means having the power to use the sword of the Spirit to fight the Lord's battles. In the Garden of Gethsemane, Peter tried to use a material sword in the power of the flesh, and he failed. At Pentecost (Acts 2), he used the Spirit's sword in the power of the Spirit, and the enemy was cut to the heart! And three thousand were captured for Christ!

Apart from prayer, the sword of the Spirit will kill but not make alive. Follow the example of the apostles: "But we will give ourselves continually to prayer, and to the ministry of the word" (Acts 6:4).

The Christian's "Keeping"

In this little letter, Jude has much to say about professed Christians who actually deny the faith and fall into judgment. But buried in this otherwise "dark" epistle are three wonderful phrases that shine like stars. They all relate to the "keeping" of the Christian life.

We are kept (preserved) in Christ (v. 1). Our salvation rests on His grace and power, not on our efforts. When He cried, "It is finished!" He settled the sin question forever. Once you have trusted in Him, you are preserved in Christ for all eternity.

We must keep ourselves in the love of God (v. 21). This does not say, "Keep yourselves saved." No, it says, "Keep yourselves in the place where your Father can love you and bless you." A disobedient child is still loved by his father, but the child is not in the place where he can *enjoy* that love. The apostle John would call this "abiding in Christ" (see John 14:21-24).

Finally, Christ will keep you from falling (v. 24). This is simply the promise of Philippians 1:6 in different words. He will keep you from falling today, and tomorrow present you faultless before His Father's throne! What He starts, He finishes.

These three "keeping" verses seem to describe the believer's past (v. 1), present (v. 21), and future (v. 24). Do they describe *your* experience today?

The Peril of Ignorance

"Ignorance is bliss!" chants the world, little realizing how stupid the statement is. Does any man want to visit a physician who is ignorant of medicine or follow a navigator who does not know the right course? Ignorance is tragedy, and that is especially true in the Christian life.

The people Christ was addressing in this church had an extremely high estimation of themselves. They were rich and self-sufficient in their own eyes. Christ told them they were bankrupt and wretched! They believed Christ was leading their church, when actually He was outside the door trying to get in!

This reminds us of Samson who got up to battle and didn't know "that the Lord was departed from him" (Judges 16:20). He had played with sin, and (as always) sin had deceived him. His power was gone!

A wise man once said, "The unexamined life is not worth living." How easy it is for us to fool ourselves, compare ourselves with others, and believe we are pleasing God. No, the best thing to do is to have an honest inventory. "Search me, O God, and know my heart: try me, and know my thoughts" (Psalm 139:23).

2 Samuel 6:1-11
John 12:1-3

". . . And Thy House"

A little boy was sitting by a stack of luggage in a hotel lobby, and a sympathetic bellhop was trying to encourage him. Apparently there had been a mix-up on the reservation for this family that had just moved to town.

"Well, don't cry," said the bellhop. "One of these days soon you'll have a home."

The boy smiled. "Oh, that's OK. We already *have* a home; all we have to do is find a house to put it in!"

Wise thinking. There's a difference between a house and a home. And there's a difference between any home and a *Christian* home. That difference is Christ.

Mary brought her gift of love to Christ's feet, and the fragrance filled the house. There is a different atmosphere to the home that gives its best to Christ. David put the ark (a symbol of Jesus Christ) in the house of Obed-edom, and turned that humble dwelling into a holy of holies. "The Lord blessed Obed-edom, and all his household" (1 Samuel 6:11).

It's wonderful for the family to attend church, but it's even better to have a church in your own house as well! Give your all—your best—to Christ, and the fragrance and blessing will be yours.

Eternal Exercise

Food and exercise go together, both in the spiritual life and the physical. Paul warned Timothy to be nourished in healthy doctrine (that's what the word *good* means here), and then to *exercise* himself unto godliness. Of course, the apostle is not condemning bodily exercise; he is simply making a comparison: spiritual exercise is good for this life and for all eternity.

Paul practiced what he preached! "Herein do I exercise myself, to have always a conscience void of offence" (Acts 24:16). The believer who feeds on the Word but who never practices it will become overweight and sluggish spiritually. This explains why the believers addressed in Hebrews 5:12-14 were in such terrible spiritual condition: they had failed to have "their senses exercised to discern both good and evil" (v. 14).

What kind of Christians would we be if we put as much enthusiasm into spiritual things as we do a golf game, a baseball game, or a bowling tournament? Professional athletes know the important part that proper diet and proper exercise play in their lives. Christians ought to be as disciplined in eternal things as the world is in temporal things!

Don't neglect your spiritual exercises today! Be a *doer* of the Word.

Leviticus 10:1-3
Isaiah 42:8

One Thing God Will Never Give You

These two sons of Aaron should have known better. They disobeyed God's word, intruded into God's presence, and tasted of God's judgment. Their "strange fire" was not acceptable to the Lord, even though they put on a good show.

God will never give His glory to another. He will *honor* the servant who honors Him (1 Samuel 2:30), but God alone must receive the glory. Because Nadab and Abihu took the glory to themselves, they incurred the wrath of God.

Someone has said, "There is no limit to what God will do for a man who will let Him have all the glory." What a challenge! Yet even in Christian service we find ourselves too often stepping into the spotlight and basking in the praise of men. Certainly Christians are to esteem their spiritual leaders highly for their work's sake (1 Thessalonians 5:12-13), but no worker must steal the glory that belongs to God alone.

Jesus said of the Holy Spirit, "He shall glorify me" (John 16:14). If we seek to glorify Christ, then the Holy Spirit will work with us. If we take the glory to ourselves, the Spirit will be grieved. God no longer sends fire from heaven to slay proud men, but He does remove His hand of blessing when we fail to glorify Him. And that is a *living* death.

When Moses Robbed God

We can understand why God would slay two priests who rashly invaded the sacred Tabernacle, but why be so hard on Moses? After all, don't most men lose their patience occasionally? And wouldn't those rebellious Jews be enough to make any leader angry?

God is no respecter of persons. In fact, the more privileges He gives a man, the more severe is that man's testing. "Unto whomsoever much is given, of him shall be much required" (Luke 12:48). Moses knew God intimately; this made his sin even greater in God's sight.

What was Moses' sin? Impatience? Anger? Self-will? Yes, all of these to some extent, but in the final analysis it was this: *failing to give God the glory.* He was not rushing into the Tabernacle; he was not breaking the Sabbath; he was simply taking to himself the honor that belonged to God. "Must *we* fetch you water out of this rock?" (Numbers 20:10, emphasis added). He was putting himself ahead of God.

Then the sentence came—not death, but loss of inheritance in the Promised Land. Moses had to wait until Jesus came, to set foot on the soil of Palestine—and then only for a brief time (Matthew 17:1-3). Sins of the disposition are dangerous because they rob God of glory. Don't rob God today!

When Unbelief Cries

God had told the people to enter and possess the land, but they preferred to spy it out just to see if God was really telling the truth! Well, He was—it was a rich land, a beautiful land, and a fruitful land. But there were giants! "We are not able to overcome!" This was the majority report.

The minority report came from Caleb and Joshua, and Moses agreed with them: "We are well able to overcome it!" This is the Old Testament version of Romans 8:31: "If God be for us, who can be against us?" The majority saw the obstacles, and they were bigger than their God. The minority saw God, and the obstacles disappeared!

Unbelief always cries and complains. It plays the same tune: "We are not able!" The nation had the promises of God to lean on and the presence of God to depend on, but they preferred to walk by sight. It cost them forty years in the wilderness, the world's longest funeral march!

Christians do not fight *for* victory; we fight *from* victory. Jesus said, "In the world ye shall have tribulation: but be of good cheer; I have overcome the world" (John 16:33). John said, "This is the victory that overcometh the world, even our faith" (1 John 5:4).

Either we are overcomers—or overcome.

When the Tables Are Turned

Nowhere does God promise to *keep us* out of troubles, but He does promise to *deliver us* out of troubles. Of course, we should not deliberately disobey Him and get ourselves into problems that only God can solve. That would be tempting God. But when our walk and our witness bring us into difficulties, God promises two things: (1) He will bring us out, and (2) He will take care of those who persecuted us.

The Bible is full of examples of this principle. Joseph's brothers sold him in envy and helped create years of suffering and trial. But God delivered Joseph and then turned the heat on his brothers. Daniel refused to stop praying, so he was thrown in the lions' den. But God delivered him, and the false accusers were thrown in to take his place. Peter was delivered from prison (Acts 12), and the guards were slain in his stead.

Now, no believer *longs* to see his persecutors punished or slain! Rather, we pray for them and seek to return good for evil. But the fact that *God is in control* is what enables us to return good for evil. No Christian takes vengeance into his own hands; the God who delivers him is able to defend him as well.

There is coming a day when the tables will be turned, and the Judge of all the earth will do what is right.

Genesis 5:23-24
Hebrews 11:5
Jude 14-15

Living in the Future

Too many people are living in the past. Enoch was a man who lived in the future. His entire biography in the Bible is wrapped up in the second coming of Jesus Christ.

Enoch preached the second coming. "The Lord cometh!" was his message, and he wanted everyone to hear it. It wasn't easy to preach to the crowd that lived before the Flood, but Enoch was faithful to his message.

Enoch practiced the second coming. He walked with God. "Every man that hath this hope in him purifieth himself, even as he is pure," states 1 John 3:3. That means that we live as though Jesus Christ may come back at any moment. John warns that some believers will be "ashamed before him at his coming" (1 John 2:28).

Enoch pictured the second coming. One day he was gone! "Translated" is the way God describes it: taken out of this world and into another world. Taken away before the terrible flood of judgment fell on the earth! "For God hath not appointed us to wrath, but to obtain salvation by our Lord Jesus Christ" (1 Thessalonians 5:9).

Start living in the future, and see how wonderful the present can become.

Contented Christians

Contentment does not mean indifference or satisfaction with things as they are. These verses talk about brotherly love, sharing the burdens and bonds of others, and opening our homes to believers in need. But only a contented Christian could do those things! Why? Because ministries like those involve sacrifice, and a man who lives for material gain will never sacrifice for others.

The secret of contentment is "I will never leave thee, nor forsake thee" (v. 5). The presence of Jesus Christ in every area and aspect of our lives gives us the peace we need in spite of sacrifices.

Take the fear of men: "The Lord is my helper, and I will not fear what man shall do unto me" (v. 6).

Take the fear of losing material things: "Be content with such things as ye have: for he hath said, I will never leave thee, nor forsake thee" (v. 5).

Covetousness and cowardice have to disappear when we practice the presence of Christ. He will supply every need; He will fight every battle. "The Lord is my helper."

Hudson Taylor used to hang two mottoes in each place where he lived: "Ebenezer—Hitherto hath the Lord helped us. Jehovah-jireh—The Lord will see to it." This is Christian contentment, the fruit of Christian companionship: "I will never leave thee, nor forsake thee."

The Blessed By-Product

Many of the commodities we use daily are actually by-products. Man's quest for oil, for example, opened up many new industries just to produce the by-products.

Christian joy is a by-product. The person who goes out to look for joy will never find it. But the Christian who wants to bear fruit for God's glory will always experience Christian joy. Joy comes from *abiding in Christ.*

We abide in Christ through the Word that cleanses us (v. 3). Spending time daily in the Word and meditating on it during the day helps to maintain that close fellowship with Christ that is so necessary to joy.

Prayer is also important (v. 7). The Word and prayer go together, of course. "But we will give ourselves continually to prayer, and to the ministry of the word," says Peter in Acts 6:4.

Loving obedience is a third condition of abiding (v. 10). Obeying the Word is evidence of our love for Christ; it is also the result of prayer and feeding on the Word.

And the result? Christian joy—a blessed by-product!

The happiest Christians are those who abide. Are you among them?

How to Open the Day

These verses speak of Jesus Christ. Verse 6 describes some of His shame and suffering at the hands of His enemies, and verse 7 shows the dedication and determination He had as He faced the cross: "He stedfastly set his face to go to Jerusalem" (Luke 9:51).

But they also give us an insight into our Lord's personal devotional life (if we may use that term). His Father awakened Him each morning, opened His ear, and taught Him the Word. What a wonderful way to begin the day!

Christ opened the day by opening His ear to God's voice. He was fed by the Word and led by the Word. What He spoke, He had first heard. "I speak to the world those things which I have heard of him [God the Father]," said Jesus (John 8:26). The effective witness is the one who first knows how to hear.

Because Jesus gave His ear to the Father, it was not difficult for Him to give His back to the smiters or His face to the scorners. "Behold, the Lord God will help me" (Isaiah 50:9). This was His confidence, and He was not disappointed. He set His face like a flint. "I have finished the work which thou gavest me to do" (John 17:4).

The way to open the day is to open your ear to hear the voice of God.

Inside Out

While Peter was writing primarily to Christian wives, telling them how to win their unsaved husbands, he was teaching all of us an important lesson: If we care for the inside, the outside will take care of itself. "The hidden man of the heart" (v. 4) —the inner man—is of far more value and ought to receive the greater attention.

Of course, Peter is not condemning a decent hairdo or attractive clothing! He is saying, "There can be no true beauty on the outside unless there is beauty on the inside." The inner person—the true self—determines the outer expression and action, and therefore ought to be carefully cultivated.

This ties in with Psalm 96:9: "O worship the Lord in the beauty of holiness." The man of the world sees no beauty in holiness, but the believer does. Just as the white light shining through the prism breaks up into the beautiful hues of the spectrum, so the holiness of God shines through the Christian and produces true beauty. The psalmist looked at Jesus Christ by faith and said, "Thou art fairer than the children of men" (Psalm 45:2). The sinner looked at Him and said, "There is no beauty that we should desire him" (Isaiah 53:2).

The same Holy Spirit who brooded over creation and brought beauty to the world wants to create that same beauty in our lives —from the inside out. Don't be an artificial Christian, depending on human adornment. Let the beauty of the Lord God be upon you!

We Don't Have to Faint

I remember one of two occasions when I fainted. It was a hot day, and I was sitting on a table in the emergency ward of the hospital. The doctor was going to tap my lung. Somewhere along the line, I felt smothered. Everything began to whirl and become gray, and I toppled over onto the table. The next thing I remembered was breathing oxygen through a face mask. That brought me through.

Prayer is to the believer what breathing oxygen is to the patient! Prayer is not a luxury; it is a necessity! No parent has to say to his children, "Now don't forget to breathe today!" Breathing is *natural* to a healthy, living creature.

If we don't pray, we faint; it's as simple as that. Prayer is our life's breath. And Jesus encourages us to pray by contrasting us to this woman in the story. That's right—it is a study in *contrasts*. She got her prayer answered in spite of all kinds of difficulties. Will not we get our needs met, *since we don't face any of the difficulties she faced?* She was a stranger coming to a judge; we are children coming to a Father. She had no promises; we have the very promises of God! She had no lawyer; we have a heavenly Advocate to intercede for us. The judge had no interest in her; our Father cares for us.

Don't give up. Don't faint. God isn't asleep or unconcerned. He will answer you when the time is right.

Three Men in a Church

Like the snowflakes and the flowers, no two Christians are alike. Of course, *all* Christians ought to be more like Christ, but this does not mean that we lose our individuality. It only means that we lose those objectionable characteristics that keep us from glorifying God.

Gaius was the man who received this brief letter, and evidently he was a fine Christian. He was in good spiritual health and able to walk in the truth. He was generous to strangers and did all he could to win souls.

And Demetrius seems to have been an equally dedicated man; all the Christians spoke well of him. Any church would benefit from having Gaius and Demetrius in the fellowship!

But Diotrephes! He was the problem. He loveth—what? Souls? The saints? The Word? No, he "loveth to have the preeminence" (v. 9). He was unwilling to be quietly at work for the Master, allowing God to receive glory. He had to be in the spotlight, telling everybody else what to do and becoming angry when things weren't done his way. How many church problems have been created by Diotrephes and his descendants!

We wonder what Diotrephes thought when the epistle to the Colossians was read in the church, especially 1:18: "That in all things he [Christ] might have the preeminence." Or Romans 12:10, "In honour preferring one another."

His Unfinished Work

The epistle to the Hebrews exalts the finished work of Christ. "By one offering he hath perfected for ever them that are sanctified" (10:14). "But this man, after he had offered one sacrifice for sins for ever, sat down on the right hand of God" (v. 12). Once you have trusted Him, the work of salvation is finished. "Their sins and iniquities will I remember no more" (v. 17).

But the finished work is the basis for the *unfinished* work —the work He performs *in us*. The good Shepherd *died* for us, and the great Shepherd *lives* for us and works in us to make us more like Himself.

His present ministry in heaven as High Priest is the chief message of chapters 6-10 of Hebrews. This is the "meat" of the Word that the spiritual babies cannot digest (5:9-14). The "milk" is the truth about His finished work on earth that is recorded in the four gospels. The "meat" deals with His present ministry through the Spirit, as explained in the epistles.

He works in us by His Spirit, and the Spirit uses the Word. As we spend time in the Word, and allow the Word to work in us, we become mature (perfect) in the Father's will. And His will *pleases* us; it isn't something we do out of fear or compulsion.

Are you experiencing this wonderful inward "unfinished work" in your life?

First Things First

Three times in the Sermon on the Mount the Lord tells us what to do first.

"First be reconciled to thy brother" (5:24). The Christian life has both horizontal and vertical responsibilities, toward God and toward men. And we cannot separate one from the other. If a man says he loves God, he will prove it by loving his brother. Jesus makes clear that the gift at the altar is of no value unless our hearts are right with each other. Our religious actions might fool men, but they will never fool God. He sees the heart.

"Seek ye first the kingdom of God" (6:33). This whole section has to do with worrying about *things*. But Jesus teaches that things cannot be at the center of life; God must be at the center. "All these things shall be *added* unto you." The things of life that we think are so important are really only additions, fringe benefits that come when we put Christ first.

"First cast out the beam out of thine own eye" (7:5). Take the two-by-four out of your own eye before trying to remove the speck from your brother's eye. In short, *don't be harder on other people than you are on yourself.* There is nothing sinful about wanting to help my brother see better, provided I have twenty-twenty vision myself.

Put first things first.

Take Care of the Temple

The believers at Corinth were having a hard time keeping clean. To begin with, many of them had lived wicked lives before being saved (vv. 9-11). And the city itself (like most cities today) was filled with temptation and wickedness. Their situation was not much different from ours.

Paul is encouraging them to keep their lives clean, and he does so by reminding them of what God has done for them.

God made their bodies; therefore they should use their bodies to glorify Him (v. 13). One day their bodies will be raised and glorified (v. 14).

Furthermore, Christ died to purchase those bodies! And now their bodies are the very members of Christ (v. 15). How can they take their bodies, the very members of Christ, and use them for sin?

And God the Holy Spirit indwells their bodies (v. 19). The believer's body is a temple, purchased by Christ and indwelt by the Spirit. Dare we to take His temple and defile it? Perish the thought!

"Ye are brought with a price"—that's the new relationship. "Therefore glorify God in your body"—that's the new responsibility. Take care of the temple; it belongs to God.

Friends and Enemies

Jesus tells us that Satan is both a liar and a murderer (John 8:44). He is the lion (1 Peter 5:8), but he is also the serpent (Revelation 12:9). In this chapter, Joshua was deceived by the enemy—the serpent—not defeated by the army.

Joshua made a mistake we all have made often; he judged according to appearances. He based his thinking on the "facts" of the case, never dreaming that the facts might be wrong. No matter how logical a man may be in his reasoning, if he begins with the wrong premises, he must reach the wrong conclusions.

They "asked not counsel at the mouth of the Lord" (Joshua 9:14). Consequently, they fell into the trap, and as a result, they had to welcome their enemies, keep peace with them, and even *defend* them. How much better it would have been to call a prayer meeting and seek the will of God. "If any of you lack wisdom, let him ask of God," promises James 1:5, "and it shall be given him."

Don't be deceived by appearances. Even Satan can masquerade as an angel of light (2 Corinthians 11:14). Take time to seek God's guidance today, or you may find yourself making friends with the enemy.

Wait for the Dawn

"Weeping may endure for a night, but joy cometh in the morning," is the gracious promise in verse 5. For the unsaved man, there is no morning; his life moves from darkness to darkness. But for the Christian, there is always the promise of morning, and "joy cometh in the morning."

The great victory of the resurrection was announced in the morning. For many hours the disciples had been weeping in darkness, and their world had collapsed. But then Jesus appeared—*alive!* "Then were the disciples glad, when they saw the Lord" (John 20:20).

Often the tragedies of this life bring weeping. Jesus never promised that we would have an easy time, that there would never be night. "All sunshine makes a desert," say the Arabs, and all blessings with no burdens make a barren life. God controls night and day; He knows just when we need some season of darkness for the cultivation of our character.

But no matter how long the darkness may hover, joy will *always* come in the morning. There will *always* be that "tomorrow" when we see the Lord and the darkness passes away.

It has often been said, but it bears repeating: never doubt in the dark what God has taught you in the light. Joy cometh in the morning.

Yes, You Can Trust Him

"God is faithful" (1 Corinthians 1:9). This was the testimony of the apostle who had gone through great trials and dangers for Christ. "Great is thy faithfulness" (Lamentations 3:23). This was the testimony of the prophet Jeremiah who watched his nation decay and finally become enslaved to the enemy.

How strange that men who have *suffered* should magnify the faithfulness of God. But how else would they learn of His faithfulness? The fact that men can trust God is not learned by reading a book or listening to a lecture. It is learned by going through the furnace, daring to rest your cause with Him.

God's faithfulness is not altered by our failures. "If we believe not, yet he abideth faithful: he cannot deny himself" (2 Timothy 2:13). God's faithfulness does not fail when our faith fails, but the failure of our faith robs us of the blessings of His promises. Don't depend on *your* faith; depend on His faithfulness.

He is faithful to forgive (1 John 1:9); He is faithful to deliver in temptation (1 Corinthians 10:13); He is faithful to keep His promises (Hebrews 10:23). Yes, you can trust Him!

Do It Again!

Here is a man who knew his history; he knew what God had done in the past *and he wanted Him to do it again!* He was tired of the status quo. (One man defined "status quo" as "the mess we're in.") He was tired of "business as usual" and "services as usual." He wanted to see something *unusual!*

What stands between us and the miracle-working power of God? For one thing, *uncleanness* (v. 6). Note that it is not our *sins* that are dirty; it is *our righteousness!* The very things we do that we think are good are evil in God's sight.

Another barrier is *unconcern* (v. 7). People just don't want to get stirred up! Most people will get worked up over an athletic event or a political contest, but very few get stirred up over spiritual things. No wonder God's power is absent from our lives and churches!

Unyieldedness is a third barrier: "Thou art the potter, I am the clay" we sing in a gospel song based on verse 8. Clay is worthless by itself, but yielded to the hands of the potter, it has great potential! *God must have His way before He will share His power.*

Don't be afraid to get stirred up. It could be the beginning of great things in your life and ministry. Lord, do it again!

It Takes Both

John the Baptist did no miracle, yet he did win souls. Lazarus preached no sermons, yet he did win souls. Lazarus *was* a miracle! People *looked at* him and trusted Christ. They *listened to* John and trusted Christ.

It takes both. "I never talk about Christ," a man once said to me. "I just let my light shine." Well, it's good to let your light shine; but if it is shining as it should, people will want to know *who lit it*. And that will be your opportunity to tell them about Jesus Christ.

The message and the miracle go together in our lives as witnesses. There was a time when we were "dead in trespasses and sins" (Ephesians 2:1), but Christ raised us from the dead. Like Lazarus, we walk "in newness of life" (Romans 6:4), and people ought to see a difference. A witness with the lips that is contradicted by the life is worse than no witness at all. "They profess that they know God; but in works they deny him" (Titus 1:16).

It is each believer's responsibility to win souls. We may not be powerful preachers like John, but we can say to lost sinners, "Behold the Lamb of God, which taketh away the sin of the world" (John 1:29). And we can walk in resurrection power so that people can see the difference in our lives. It takes both —and Christ makes both possible.

The Power of a Touch

This woman had a hidden need that those around her knew nothing about. You may have a hidden need too. She had tried every available means to meet her need, but nothing succeeded. Mark 5:26 tells us she had spent all her money and was only growing worse. What a terrible condition to be in!

She admitted her need and came to Jesus. She could have said, "Nothing else worked," "It isn't right to come to Jesus last," or perhaps made some other excuse, but she didn't. She came to Him in spite of the crowd and in spite of the fact that He was on His way to the home of Jairus to heal his daughter.

Never be afraid to come to Jesus. He is never too busy! And don't measure your faith; just start with faith that you have and lay hold of the hem of His garment. You have to start *somewhere!* A man does not have to be a learned theologian to experience the power of God in his life. This woman's faith was almost superstitious, yet Christ honored it.

We have to be willing to lay aside our excuses. We must forget the failures of the past. We must press through the crowd to Jesus and by faith take hold of Him. He will do the rest. Never underestimate the power of a touch of faith.

Take Care of Your Ears

Your ears are the most important organs you have, spiritually speaking. "Faith cometh by hearing, and hearing by the word of God" (Romans 10:17). Often, Jesus cried, "He that hath ears to hear, let him hear!"

Two warnings are in order. The first comes from Mark: "Take heed *what* ye hear" (4:24, emphasis added). Why? Because what you hear determines what you become. What you hear is what you receive, and what you receive determines what you have to give to others. The second warning is from Luke: "Take heed therefore *how* ye hear" (8:18, emphasis added). We can hear the right things, but if we don't hear them in the right way they will do us no good. Careless hearing leads to careless loving.

We often complain about "dull preachers," but Hebrews 5:11 tells us that some Christians are *dull hearers*. They have listened to the noise of this world and lost their ability to hear the voice of God! Paul warns us in 2 Timothy 4:3-4 that some people will develop "itching ears," wanting to hear man's exciting new ideas instead of God's eternal Word. But even this will grow old, and they will finally turn away their ears from the truth.

Take heed *what* you hear. Be careful to hear only that which is true and wholesome. When you find something worth hearing, then take heed *how* you hear. Ear trouble creates heart trouble.

The High Cost of a Song

Popular entertainers command huge fees just for singing or playing a few songs. It really costs them little to sing the song, yet the public has to pay the bill.

Think of what it cost Mary to be able to sing her song of praise: "Behold the handmaid of the Lord; be it unto me according to thy word" (v. 38). She had to surrender her all, yield her body to the Lord, and then she could sing. Hers was no *borrowed* song; it came from her heart, and it expressed her faith. This is the kind of song that really counts.

"When the burnt offering began, the song of the Lord began also" (2 Chronicles 29:27). The principle is clear: first the sacrifice, then the song. And this principle runs all the way through the Bible. Many of the songs of David recorded in the Psalms were written out of great suffering and sacrifice. Paul and Silas suffered at the hands of the Philippian officials, yet they were able to enjoy "songs in the night."

Of course, as in everything, Jesus is the supreme Example. He shared the broken bread and the cup with His disciples—picturing His body given on the cross. His blood shed for sinners —*and then He sang a hymn!*

If you have lost the song in your life, perhaps it is because you have forgotten the sacrifice.

Poor Posture

I don't recommend skipping through a Bible book in this fashion, but I'm doing so to emphasize a point. All of these verses emphasize the believer's "spiritual posture."

Once you were lying in the grave, dead in trespasses and sins. Then, by the grace of God, you were raised, *not* to sit on the tombstone but to sit with Christ in the heavenlies! Where a man sits determines what he can do. No matter where the President of the United States may be *physically* (on a golf course, in a jet), he exercises power because of where he sits by authority—behind the President's desk and in the President's chair.

So with the Christian: we have spiritual authority because we sit with Christ in the heavenlies. This wonderful position moves us to another posture: we *bow the knee* to Christ and seek His blessing in prayer. This, in turn, makes it possible for us to *walk* daily so as to please Him, and it enables us to *stand* against the attacks of Satan.

Poor physical posture can cause all kinds of problems. Poor spiritual posture is the source of most of our spiritual problems. Perhaps it's time to visit the great Physician and have your posture checked.

The "Whatness" of Witness

Christians are supposed to be witnesses, not prosecuting attorneys. It is not our responsibility to tell people their faults and sins; it is our privilege to tell them about Christ and the salvation He alone can give. Like the shepherds and the apostles, our task is simply to tell people what we have seen and heard concerning Jesus Christ.

This makes witnessing a personal, practical thing. Some Christians "play the same old record" and believe they are communicating the excitement and challenge of the Christian life, but they're not. Unless we walk daily with Christ in a real experience, we have nothing to share with others. The gospel is not only past history (although it is certainly based on historical facts); it is present reality. "That which we have seen and heard declare we unto you, that ye also may have fellowship with us" (1 John 1:3).

If witnessing means sharing a personal experience, then the believer must maintain that fellowship. The indwelling Holy Spirit makes Christ real *to* us, and then *through* us to others. "But when the Comforter is come . . . ," said Jesus, "he shall testify of me: and ye also shall bear witness, because ye have been with me from the beginning" (John 15:26-27).

Don't allow witnessing to become a strained, artificial thing. Yield to the Spirit, enjoy a personal walk with Christ, and like the disciples, you will say, "We cannot but speak the things which we have seen and heard" (Acts 4:20).

Blessings and Cursings

Nehemiah reaches back into history to recall the story of Balaam, the false prophet who tried to curse Israel. But God turned the curse into a blessing!

Only God can do that. Joseph thought he was under a curse when he was sold into Egypt as a slave, but God turned the curse into a blessing, and Joseph saved his family. Paul's thorn in the flesh seemed to be a curse, but it too was turned into a blessing. Even the crown of thorns that Jesus wore was transmuted into a crown of glory!

But the reverse is also true: God can turn our blessings into curses. The priests in Malachi's day were bored with their religious faith; they were giving God second best. Instead of being faithful to their covenant, they disobeyed the Word openly. God warned them: "The very blessings that you enjoy will become curses to you if you disobey Me!" Examples of this judgment are not hard to find: God can take health, money, family, and even friends, and turn them into curses if we fail to obey His Word.

Christ was made a curse for us that He might be able to turn our curses into blessings.

Stones for the Building

You would expect Peter to call believers "living stones," since his name means "a rock." Christians are not *dead* stones, but *living* stones; and they received that life by being born into God's family ("newborn babes," v. 2). Christ is *the stone*, of course, and Christians are living stones built up into a holy temple for the Lord.

Christ has a plan for His building. Since He purchased the stones at the cost of His own blood (1 Peter 1:18-19), He has the right to place them where He pleases. *A stone that is out of place ceases to be a stone and becomes a stumbling block*. Because the Jewish nations would not give Christ His rightful place, they stumbled over Him, and it brought judgment.

Christ must be in His proper place of preeminence, and we must be in our proper place of service, if the temple is to grow and be strong. What a privilege to be a living stone in His temple! What a tragedy to be out of place!

To the lost world, Christ is not precious; He is rejected. But to the believer, Christ is precious, the precious stone on whom our hopes for time and eternity rest. When He loses that preciousness in our lives, we cease to glorify Him. "Precious" seems like a strange word from the lips of a fisherman, but that was the only word Peter would use!

Is that stone precious to you?

The Church God Sees

The church at Corinth was having problems. There were divisions and disagreements among the members; there was disgrace because of the way some of them were living; there were even debate and drunkenness at their meetings! Paul tried to solve these problems by reminding the church *what it really was in the eyes of God:* a family (vv. 1-4), a garden (vv. 5-9), and a temple (vv. 10-17).

The local church is a family, and not all the members are as mature as they should be. Some are still "babes in Christ" (v. 1), and they need (or demand) a great deal of attention. They argue and quarrel because they want their own way. The remedy? Feed them the Word of God so they will grow up!

The church is also a garden. "Ye are God's husbandry" (v. 9) means "Ye are God's cultivated field, God's garden." What an eye-opening comparison! The seed is God's Word; the preachers and teachers are sowers and cultivators, but only God can give the increase. The fruit that we harvest depends on the kind of seed that we sow. Proverbs 6:19 reminds us that God hates the man who "soweth discord among brethren."

And the church is a temple, built on the solid rock, Christ Jesus. We cannot change the foundation, but we can use the wrong materials in building. It takes patience and hard work to get gold, silver, and jewels; it takes little effort to find wood, hay, and stubble. But which will last the longest?

Take time to evaluate your own place in your local church. It will help your church—*and you!*

God's Medicine

"You can hardly find a doctor who will make house calls!" a friend said to me recently. "If I'm well enough to go to the office, I don't need him!"

All of us sympathize with the overworked doctors, but we rejoice that our *spiritual* medicine is not so difficult to secure. The great Physician makes house calls; He brings the Word of God and applies it to our lives.

Sin cuts and destroys, but God's Word (like medicine) heals and builds up. All we have to do is admit the need and ask Him to meet it. Of course, there are always the "quack cures" that people recommend, but these are dangerous. "They have healed also the hurt of the daughter of my people slightly, saying, Peace, Peace; when there is no peace" (Jeremiah 6:14). Superficial examinations and superficial remedies only make the patient worse.

The medicine of the Word, like any medicine, must be taken *by faith*. It was this mistake that kept Israel out of the Promised Land: "But the word preached did not profit them, not being mixed with faith in them that heard it" (Hebrews 4:2). "According to your faith be it unto you" (Matthew 9:29).

Take your medicine!

The Difference Between Life and Death

There is a grand canyon of difference between repentance and remorse. Peter repented, and Christ forgave him; Judas showed remorse and went out and hung himself. Paul explained it this way: "For godly sorrow worketh repentance to salvation ... but the sorrow of the world worketh death" (2 Corinthians 7:10).

Remorse is sorrow I experience because I made a mistake and was caught. Repentance is much deeper; it is sorrow I experience because I have sinned against Christ and hurt Him. "The Lord turned, and looked upon Peter" (Luke 22:61). That look was enough to break Peter's heart and bring him to repentance.

It is one thing to *confess* sin (even Judas did that) but quite another to *judge* sin. Judas became his own judge and jury rather than face the judgment of God—*and he faced it anyway!* Peter, on the other hand, accepted the judgment of God and therefore experienced the mercy of God.

Our heart's attitude toward sin makes the difference between life and death.

Whom Are You Trusting Today?

All men have faith; all men trust something or someone. The difference between the Christian and the non-Christian is not that one has faith and the other one does not. Rather, the Christian puts his faith *in Christ,* whereas the non-Christian trusts himself "and maketh flesh his arm" (v. 5).

The results are opposite: the man who trusts himself turns his life into a desert; the man who trusts the Lord becomes like a fruitful tree. Again, the difference is in the *roots:* the Christian spreads his roots out by "the river" (v. 8) and draws in the spiritual nourishment that the Spirit supplies. The non-Christian is rooted in himself, and there is no nourishment there.

Why would a man deliberately reject the life of faith for the life of self-effort and drought? *Because his heart is deceived.* He actually believes that his life is a paradise, when it is really a desert! Sin has so corrupted his tastes and blinded his eyes that he is unable to make honest judgments. Sin is killing him, yet he believes he is "really living!" This is what Hebrews 3:13 means by "the deceitfulness of sin."

Whose arm are you trusting today: your arm, or God's?

Genesis 13:5-18
James 4:1-4

The Two Wars

Of all disagreements that may come to our lives, family disagreements are the worst. "Behold, how good and how pleasant it is for brethren to dwell together in unity!" sings the psalmist (133:1). But Lot's men were fighting with Abraham's men, and the situation was neither good nor pleasant.

The real trouble lay in Lot's heart. *There has to be war on the inside before there can be war on the outside.* James hit the nail on the head: Lot was worldly minded (he wanted the riches of Sodom), and he did not take time to pray for the will of the Lord. His friendship with the world made him an enemy of God and, consequently, an enemy of Abraham. "Can two walk together, except they be agreed?" (Amos 3:3).

Abraham handled the matter beautifully: he allowed Lot to make the first choice. Abraham, by faith, was "detached" from the things of this world; he was living by the promises of God, walking by faith, not by sight. *And God rewarded him for it.* Lot received his little piece of real estate, but God gave Abraham *the entire land!*

"Ye cannot serve God and mammon" (Matthew 6:24). "A double minded man is unstable in all his ways" (James 1:8). Settle the war on the inside, and there will be no wars on the outside.

It Works Both Ways

Everybody knows John 3:16; but 1 John 3:16 seems to be forgotten. It is a masterpiece of divine logic: if God loved us, we ought to love one another. If He gave Himself for us, we ought to give ourselves to others.

It is not enough to say that we have *experienced* the love of God; we must also *express* that love. The same Holy Spirit who revealed God's love *to* me will shed that love abroad *through* me to touch the lives of others. "Because the love of God is shed abroad in our hearts by the Holy Ghost which is given unto us" (Romans 5:5).

This love is practical; it is a matter of deeds, not words. Jesus didn't just talk about the cross; He actually made the sacrifice. Christians don't just talk about love; they too make the sacrifice. *Unless there is a sacrifice, there is no love*.

The more we experience the love of God, the more we will love others. And the more we love others, the more we will experience the love of God! It works both ways.

He Already Knows

"Jesus prevented him" (v. 25) simply means Jesus anticipated him; He knew the need already. And that's the way Jesus is; He knows our needs and has the answer ready. "It shall come to pass, that before they call, I will answer," promises Isaiah 65:24.

Jesus is concerned about the practical needs of our lives. This Temple tax was not a great amount, but at the time it was too much for the disciples to pay. No doubt Peter's active mind was thinking up a solution to their problem when he went into the house. But Jesus already had the answer.

God supplies our needs because we are children of the King. "But my God shall supply all your need according to his riches in glory by Christ Jesus" (Philippians 4:19). To the tax collectors, Peter looked like a poor fisherman who was following an unemployed carpenter. But Peter was a child in God's family, and that made him rich.

If God already knows our needs and has a way to meet them, then why pray? Because prayer is God's appointed means for getting these needs met. He has the answer before we call, yet He still says, "Ye lust, and have not . . . because ye ask not" (James 4:2). Knowing that He already has the answer is an encouragement for us to pray more, not less! "Call unto me, and I will answer thee" (Jeremiah 33:3).

The Light That Never Fails

The special priestly blessing certainly has a spiritual application to believers today. In Christ, God has certainly blessed us with all spiritual blessings (Ephesians 1:3), and He is able to keep us (Jude 24). We have experienced His grace and His peace. But in one sense, we have advanced beyond the Old Testament saint: God's light does not simply shine *upon* us; it shines *within* us.

Paul seems to be comparing the conversion experience to the creation account in Genesis 1. Once our lives were "without form, and void; and darkness was upon the face of the deep" (v. 2). The Spirit of God began to work; we put faith in Christ. God said, "Let there be light" (v. 3). And the light of salvation shone into our hearts. We became new creations in Christ.

This light shines upon us and within us, and it ought to shine *through us*. "Let your light so shine before men, that they may see your good works, and glorify your Father which is in heaven" (Matthew 5:16). As Stephen faced the angry council, they "saw his face as it had been the face of an angel" (Acts 6:15). The light was shining through.

We live in a dark world. Many man-made lights are flickering and going out. Christ has given us the light that never fails. May we not fail!

119

What God Has Joined Together

"Thou hast also found grace in my sight" (v. 12); "I beseech thee, shew me thy glory" (v. 18). Grace and glory! "The Lord will give grace and glory" (Psalm 84:11). These two words are united in the Bible, and they ought to be united in our Christian experience.

Whatever begins with grace will ultimately lead to glory. Whatever begins with man's self-efforts will ultimately lead to shame. Salvation is by grace (Ephesians 2:8-10), and God has saved us "to the praise of the glory of his grace" (Ephesians 1:6). Grace and glory! And one day we shall *see* His glory and *share* His glory for all eternity.

But grace and glory are joined together in our Christian living and service as well. Paul experienced a thorn in the flesh and asked God to remove it. God's answer was, "My grace is sufficient for thee" (2 Corinthians 12:9). Paul's response was, "Most gladly therefore will I rather glory in my infirmities." Grace and glory!

He is the "God of all grace" (1 Peter 5:10). "He giveth more grace," James promised (4:6). And whatever begins with God's grace will ultimately lead to God's glory. Grace today is ours for the asking.

The Heart of the Matter

Many Christians worry about this matter of witnessing. "Am I really able to give an answer to those who ask me about Christ? Can I defend the hope I have in Him?" Well, the place to begin your preparation is not the head but the heart. "Set Jesus Christ apart as Lord in your heart!" When He rules in our lives, then the right witness will follow. "Out of the abundance of the heart the mouth speaketh" (Matthew 12:34).

Peter is dealing with false accusations against Christians. In his day, the Romans believed all sorts of strange things about believers, lies that the enemy had invented. "Don't be afraid of their accusations or their questions," Peter in essence wrote. "If Christ is Lord in your hearts, and if your conscience is clean, you have nothing to fear."

A prepared heart is the secret of a powerful life. "Keep thy heart with all diligence; for out of it are the issues of life" (Proverbs 4:23). A consecrated heart and a clean conscience are terrible weapons in the hands of the Lord. A prepared heart will lead to a pungent witness, a witness that will never leave you ashamed. It is not by thinking up arguments that we witness to the lost, but by living a life with Christ as Lord. Solomon had the same idea. Read Proverbs 22:17-21—and then practice it.

Friend or Enemy?

The Philippian letter was filled with joy and rejoicing, but here is one place where the apostle *weeps*. What is he weeping over? Over professed Christians who were really the enemies of God!

Their description isn't very beautiful. Instead of glorying in the cross as Paul did (Galatians 6:14), they gloried in their shame; they bragged about their sinful lives! They didn't live for spiritual things; their god was their belly—they lived for the flesh. They were "earthly minded" in contrast to Christians who set their affections on things above (Colossians 3:2) because their "citizenship" is in heaven (Philippians 3:20).

The cross is God's test. If we agree with the cross, then God is our friend. If we disagree, then God is our enemy. The cross means death to the flesh (Galatians 5:24) and separation from the world (Galatians 6:14). The people over whom Paul was weeping lived for the world and the flesh. No wonder they were God's enemies!

If the cross embarrasses you, or if you hide from the cross, then there is something wrong with your spiritual life. If you glory in the cross, and in the Christ of the cross, and if you are willing to bear the shame of the cross for His sake, then you will be God's friend, and He will honor you. There will be a price to pay, of course, but it will be worth it all when Jesus returns.

The earthly minded people are heading for destruction. The heavenly minded people who glory in the cross are heading for glory.

He Does It All

Verses 6-8 are a great summary of what Christ does for the man who calls on Him and trusts Him.

He saves! "This poor man cried, and the Lord heard him, and saved him out of all his troubles" (v. 6). This *poor* man. Is there any other kind of man? "For all have sinned, and *come short* of the glory of God" (Romans 3:23, emphasis added). This same word is found in Luke 15:14: "He [the prodigal son] began to be in want." When the poor sinner calls on Christ, *He saves.*

And *He keeps!* "The angel of the Lord encampeth round about them that fear him, and delivereth them" (Psalm 34:7). Jesus told the Father, "Those that thou gavest me I have kept, and none of them is lost" (John 17:12). If He was able to keep His own while He was on earth, can He not still keep them as He reigns in heaven?

And *He satisfies!* "O taste and see that the Lord is good" (Psalm 34:8). Once we have found Him, we stop our seeking, because He is all that we need. "Lord, to whom shall we go?" asks Peter in John 6:68. "Thou hast the words of eternal life." Once you have "tasted the good word of God" (Hebrews 6:5), you will have no appetite for the garbage of this world.

No wonder the psalmist *blesses* the Lord (Psalm 34:1) and *boasts* in the Lord (v. 2). With this kind of salvation, a man ought to have a song. And He does it all!

Look Alive!

"Loose him, and let him go" (John 11:44). Lazarus is *alive* now, and a living man doesn't wear grave clothes!

Paul puts it another way: "But now ye also *put off* all these" (Colossians 3:8, emphasis added), and he names the dirty grave clothes that belong to the old life. Changing clothes does not save the sinner; only the grace of God can do that. But once the dead sinner is made alive, *he wants to look alive!* No one would believe that Lazarus was alive if he still wore the grave clothes and smelled of death.

But don't stop there. Paul essentially goes on to say, "Now, put on the 'grace clothes!' " And he names some of the lovely garments of grace that belong in the wardrobe of every Christian: "mercies, kindness, humbleness of mind, meekness, long-suffering" (v. 12). And these clothes carry with them, not the fragrance of death, but the fragrance "of life unto life" (2 Corinthians 2:16).

What kind of garments are you wearing on your inner man?

Do you look alive?

Divided We Fall

Stability is a mask of maturity. Little children fall easily; mature men learn how to walk and stand. "That we henceforth be no more children, tossed to and fro, and carried about with every wind of doctrine" (Ephesians 4:14). As we grow in grace, we grow in Christian stability. James warns us that a divided mind will rob us of stability. The problem here is not false doctrine but the trials and testings that come to the life of every true Christian. When trials appear, we're prone to ask, "Why did *this* happen?" James tells us to ask God for the wisdom to understand our trials so we can make trials work *for* us and not *against* us. "Tribulation worketh patience; and patience, experience," states Romans 5:3-4. Trials build Christian character, and this means Christian stability.

Wavering faith is an indication of a double mind. A double mind is a dangerous mind because it will lead to a fall. Keep your mind fixed on the Word of God and the grace of God, and you will never fall. "This one thing I do," Paul testifies in Philippians 3:13. No divided mind here! No wonder he could face danger and say, "But none of these things move me" (Acts 20:24).

What life does *to* you, it has been said, depends on what life finds *in* you. If it finds in you a single mind, it can only make you stronger. If it finds a double mind, you are destined to fall.

From Start to Finish

Alpha and *Omega* are, of course, the first and last letters in the Greek alphabet. Christ is the beginning and the ending, the first and the last. What He starts, He finishes!

In one sense, salvation is a finished transaction, a once-for-all birth that brings you into the family of God. But in another sense, it is a lifelong process. It is "the good work" that God does in us. God starts it, God continues it, and God finishes it. "For it is God which worketh in you," says Philippians 2:13.

Our Christian experience today is really just the beginning. There is more to come! Christ, the living Word, wants to spell out in our lives the complete alphabet of His blessings, from Alpha to Omega. He is the "author and finisher of our faith" (Hebrews 12:2). Our confidence is not in ourselves, for human nature rarely finishes what it starts. Our confidence is in Him.

All the treasures of God's wisdom and knowledge are hidden in Christ (Colossians 2:3). These treasures are spelled out by the living Word in the written Word: He is the divine alphabet that unlocks the revelation of God. The more we allow Him to work in us, the more we appropriate the treasures He purchased for us. And the best is yet to come!

The Worst Kind of Blindness

This Pharisee was spiritually blind. He did not see Christ; He did not see the woman; he did not see himself.

Let's start with the last item: he did not see himself. Like most of the Pharisees, he considered himself righteous and obedient. True, he had not been guilty of the sins the woman had committed (at least not outwardly), but he was guilty of neglect. With her, it was sins of commission; with him, it was sins of omission. He had invited Jesus in and then completely ignored Him.

He did not really see the woman. He saw her past; Jesus saw her present and future. He knew her reputation; Jesus knew her faith. She was not saved by her love or her tears; they were but evidences of the faith that had saved her and given her peace.

Simon did not see Jesus. "This man, if he were a prophet . . ." (v. 39). Yet Jesus saw right into Simon's heart and revealed the sin that was there! Simon was as spiritually bankrupt as the woman ("they had nothing to pay," v. 42), yet he would not turn to Christ for that frank forgiveness.

"For judgment I am come into this world," says Jesus in John 9:39, "that they which see not might see; and that they which see might be made blind." This is the worst kind of blindness.

What We Have Is All We Need

The epistle to the Hebrews was written to people who were accustomed to *having* things they could see and feel: a Temple, an altar for sacrifices, a high priest in beautiful robes. But now they were Christians, and they had lost all that. Their Jewish neighbors would taunt them: "Where is your Temple? Where is your high priest?"

Of course, all of those Jewish things perished when Jerusalem fell to the Romans in A.D. 70. But the possessions of the Christians were untouched! Their Holy of Holies was *in heaven*, not on earth; their High Priest was *in heaven* too. And they had "a better and an enduring substance" in heaven (v. 34). And what they had was all that they needed.

Having these heavenly possessions that are eternal, we may have boldness. We need not live on the fringes; we can come straight to the throne of grace and receive what we need. There is no need to forsake our fellowship, and there is no need to fear or waver. *What we have in heaven can never be taken from us*, and what we have is all we need.

Don't build your life on the passing things of this world. Build it on the eternal possessions you have in heaven, and it can never be taken from you.

A Worm with Teeth

These words were given to encourage the Jews as they left Babylonian captivity to return to Palestine. Surrounded by hostile Gentile nations, the Jews were naturally fearful of the journey. This is why God repeatedly says, "Fear not" (41:10, 13-14; 43:1, 5; 44:2, 8).

They were a feeble people; in fact, God compares them to a *worm!* Who ever heard of a worm threshing a mountain into dust? But with the help of the Lord, that is exactly what they did.

We face many mountains in our lives, and usually we feel like feeble, helpless worms. In ourselves we can do nothing, but yielded to God we can become mighty instruments for His glory. Gideon was just a worm, but God gave him teeth to conquer the Midianites. David was just a worm, but God used him to kill a giant and deliver his nation. The early church had neither money nor political power, yet they filled Jerusalem with the gospel.

Worms—worms with teeth! Is this too low a station for us? Are we too strong, too proud to become worms? If so, then we don't have the attitude our Lord had, for Jesus confessed on the cross, "I am a worm, and no man" (Psalm 22:6).

When we are weak, He is strong. Worms can become sharp threshing tools if they are weak enough for God.

A Present Promise

Please don't apply verse 9 to heaven! Although it may include heaven, the promise is for the here and now, not the sweet by-and-by. Verse 10 makes this clear: "But God hath revealed them [these things that God has prepared] unto us by his Spirit."

The Bible takes on a new look when you realize that it contains the key to all the treasures Christ purchased for you on the cross. These precious spiritual blessings can never be understood by the natural (unsaved) man; he believes they are foolish. They must be revealed to us by the Spirit through the Word.

Spiritual discernment of spiritual things does not come to the believer automatically. This discernment is the result of discipline, obedience, and a searching of the Word. This treasure must be sought as a miner seeks silver and gold (Proverbs 2:4). Your Bible contains *all spiritual treasures*. The Holy Spirit longs to lead you into those treasures that you might possess them and enjoy them—if you will pay the price.

God has prepared for you wonderful spiritual blessings for *each day*. Don't wait until you get to heaven to claim them. Start now.

The Things That Matter Most

Most of the people we know are living in verse 2—spending money for that which is not bread, for that which cannot satisfy. They are living on substitutes, and the substitute is never as good as the real thing. They don't know the difference between prices and values. They have the things that money can buy, but not the things that money can't buy.

God wants to give away *free* that which men cannot purchase with money. A man can buy sleep but not rest; he can buy a house but not a home. He can purchase entertainment but never lasting pleasure and joy. The things that matter most are all found in Jesus Christ.

A man must forsake his own thoughts if he is going to find satisfaction in Christ. The gospel is totally contrary to the thinking of men today. The wisdom of this world is foolishness with God. God's ways are higher and God's thoughts are higher, and until men admit that they cannot be saved.

Verses 12-13 describe the transformation that takes place in the life that discovers in Christ the things that matter most. Do they describe *your* life?

We Win By Losing

Jacob's past was catching up with him. He had sinned against his brother Esau, and now Esau was approaching with a large company. What should a man do when his past is about to overtake him?

He should stop fighting and leave the matter with God!

Jacob tried to pacify Esau with his gifts and please God with his prayers, and the scheme just wouldn't work. Had Jacob yielded earlier that evening, God would have given him the victory earlier; but Jacob persisted in fighting. Finally God had to weaken him physically so He could break him. That was the turning point.

When a man lives to please men, he is always at war. When a man lives to please God, he is at peace because God will fight his battles for him. It has well been said, "Faith is living without scheming." Jacob had to start limping before he would start trusting.

God worked everything out! Esau came as a friend, not an enemy! There was no danger after all. How foolish we are to wrestle with God when yielding by faith will win the battle for us.

It Is Finished

"Is there any unfinished business?" This question is usually heard in a business meeting, but it has a proper place in the life of the Christian. Jesus was able to say, "I have finished the work which thou gavest me to do" (John 17:4). Paul wrote in his final letter, "I have finished my course" (2 Timothy 4:7).

An old author wrote, "It is always difficult to do anything for the last time." This was Paul's last letter. Soon he would move off the scene and Timothy would have to take his place. Then Timothy would be gone and another would have to step in.

The church is always one generation short of extinction. The older saints must deposit the truth of the Word with the younger saints, and they, in turn, must protect it and pass it on to others. No Christian is required to do everything; all God asks of him is that he be faithful to finish the work given him to do during his life. Moses finished his work, and Joshua took over; Elijah laid down the mantle, and Elisha took it up.

Find out where your place is and what your work is, and be faithful to do it. Then you can claim Paul's "henceforth" promise and look forward to meeting the Lord with joy and not with grief.

Where Does God Live?

When Andrew and John first met Jesus Christ, they asked Him a logical question. They wanted to know where He lived. His gracious reply was, "Come and see" (John 1:39). He gave them more than information; He gave them an invitation to a personal relationship with God! The meeting they had with Him that day completely changed their lives.

Where *does* God dwell? In the highest heavens, of course, but also *in the hearts of those who are humble before Him*. God still resists the proud but gives grace to the humble (James 4:6). When He finds a penitent and believing heart, He moves in. The God of the universe finds Himself "at home" in the life of the humblest child of God who makes room for Him.

If we love God and obey His Word, Jesus explained, then the Father and the Son will come to us and make their home with us. The word *abode* in John 14:23 is the same as "mansions" ("abiding places") in 14:2. In other words, we can experience a "heaven on earth" *while we are waiting to go to heaven!*

Can others find God at *our* address?

Come! Come! Come!

"Come and see!" was our Lord's invitation to Andrew and John, two religious men who were seeking salvation (John 1:39). They had heard John the Baptist preach and had seen him point to "the Lamb of God, which taketh away the sin of the world" (v. 29). As devout Jews, they knew all about sacrificial lambs, but they had never seen a Lamb that could save the whole world. They met Jesus, abode with Him that day, and became new men. Then they went out and won others to Christ.

But "Come and see!" is just the beginning. Jesus also said, "Come unto me, and drink" (John 7:37). He provides for us "rivers of living water" (v. 38) that flow in and through us and bring abundant life. We *become* Christians by trusting the Savior, but we *live like* Christians only through the power of the Spirit of God.

"Come and dine" is our Lord's third invitation (21:12). Jesus turned the disciples' night of disappointment into a morning of success, and then He invited the men to have breakfast with Him. Each morning, Jesus invites His people to feast with Him in His Word and find the strength that they need for the demands of life. He alone is able to sustain us and enable us, and He invites us to join Him each day.

Jesus says, "Come!"

We should say, "I will arise and go!"

God Leads the Way

Psalm 19 is a beautiful explanation of how God reveals Himself to people and guides them in His way.

To begin with, He reveals Himself in *creation* (vv. 1-6). As men look at the world above them and around them, they should realize that there is a Creator, a God who made everything. The "voice" of God's creation is a universal voice, seen by all, *and it never has to be translated into other tongues!* No one on earth can ever argue at the last judgment, "God did not reveal Himself to me."

But God further reveals Himself in *Scripture* (vv. 7-11). Creation is limited and cannot reveal everything about God. The universe shows that God exists and that He is wise and powerful, but the Holy Scriptures tell us what this God is like and what He wants to do for all who will trust Him.

God's third revelation is *in the human heart* (vv. 12-14), where God comes to meet with us as we trust Him. Knowing the glories of creation and the wonders of the Word is not enough. We must open our hearts to the Savior and allow Him to forgive us of our sins.

The Wise Men (Magi) from the East had this kind of a spiritual experience. First, they saw God's revelation in the heavens and they followed the light God gave them. This led them to the Word of God as written in the prophets, and the Word of God led them to Jesus.

Don't stop short. Like the Wise Men, keep going until you meet the Son of God personally and bow and worship Him.

Where is the Glory?

When the Bible talks about "the glory of God," it is referring to the sum total of all His attributes, all that God is and all that God does. "Glory" is not a single characteristic of God; *everything* about God is glorious. Wherever He is present, His glory is there.

God's glory originally dwelt in the Holy of Holies of the Jewish Tabernacle, where the sacred Ark of the Covenant resided. His throne was the mercy seat, that golden covering of the ark on which the sacrificial blood was sprinkled on the annual Day of Atonement.

But Israel sinned, and the glory departed from the Tabernacle. Then Solomon built the Temple, and God's glory graciously moved in. But, alas, Israel sinned again. God not only removed His glory from the Temple, *He removed the Temple from the earth.* As He chastened His disobedient people, God permitted the Babylonians to destroy Jerusalem and the Temple.

The glory returned to earth in the body of God's Son, Jesus Christ. "We beheld his glory" (John 1:14). That glory was covered in darkness when He died for us at Calvary, but He arose from the dead, and He has gone back to heaven, the glorified Son of God.

Where is the glory? Now it dwells in the lives of His people! We are His temple! Can others see His glory in us, or must God write over *our* lives, "Ichabod . . . the glory is departed" (1 Samuel 4:21)?

Genesis 39:7-12
Nehemiah 6:10-11
1 Timothy 6:1-11
2 Timothy 2:22

Know When to Run

There are times when running away is the mark of a coward, but running away can also be the mark of a wise and courageous man.

Nehemiah refused to flee, and God honored him for staying on the job and finishing the work he was called to do. Had Nehemiah become frightened, he would have run away; and then the work of rebuilding Jerusalem would have come to a halt.

But Joseph was just as courageous *when he fled from temptation.* An old Puritan writer said, "Joseph lost his coat, but he kept his character."

Paul warns us to flee the love of money, and to flee a style of life that suggests, "If you are godly, you will be rich." God does permit some of His children to be rich, but a dedicated life is no guarantee of wealth. Paul cautions us to "flee youthful lusts" (2 Timothy 2:22), and a person does not have to be young to have "youthful lusts"! Like Joseph, there are times when the best thing for us to do is run.

It's always too soon to quit God's work. But when it comes to temptation, *you can't run away fast enough!*

Are You Searching for Your Sins?

God completely and finally settled the sin question when Jesus died for you on the cross. "It is finished!" was His cry; and when you trust Him as your Savior, He forgives your sins and takes them out of the picture completely. "Their sins and iniquities will I remember no more" (Hebrews 10:17).

But Satan accuses us and wants us to remember our sins. How sad it is when God's children remember what He has forgotten—and forget what He wants us to remember!

If you start to search for your sins, where will you look?

If you look *above you*, you won't find them; because God's mercy reaches above the heavens. If you look *around you*, you won't find them; because they have been taken away "as far as the east is from the west" (Psalm 103:12). You can measure from north to south, but not from east to west!

If you look *behind you*, you will never find your sins; because God has put them behind His back. And you certainly won't find them *below you*, because your sins are buried in the depths of the sea!

So, stop searching! God has forgiven you *all* your trespasses (Colossians 2:13), and there is no one in heaven, on earth, or even in hell, who can accuse or condemn you (Romans 8:31-39).

Hallelujah, what a Savior!

Judges 18:1
Psalm 47:4
Acts 20:32
Ephesians 1:3, 11
1 Peter 1:3-5

How to Receive An Inheritance

What a tragedy that the tribe of Dan failed to claim their God-given inheritance and set out to take another tribe's inheritance by force. The Danites knew that God had arranged their inheritance for them, yet they refused to act by faith.

It is still true that God chooses our inheritance for us. He always knows what is best for His children. We may believe that the grass is greener somewhere else, but it is not. The pastures are best in those places where the Good Shepherd leads us.

Those who have been born again, through faith in Jesus Christ, have a wonderful inheritance that can never fade or lose its value. It is an inheritance that no one can steal from them, because it is reserved in heaven. You don't have to go to heaven, however, to start enjoying the inheritance Christ purchased for you; you ought to be enjoying it now!

The Word of God is the "divine bank book" that tells you how rich you are in Jesus Christ. Faith in God's gracious Word and obedience to Him will make it possible for you to claim all that you have in Jesus Christ. You don't have to be like the Danites and take your inheritance by treachery and force. You can take it by truth and faith.

Start to claim your inheritance today!

Zephaniah 3:17
Matthew 26:30
Luke 15:22-24
Ephesians 5:18-19
Hebrews 2:12

Our God Sings!

In a lyrical passage that describes God's chastened people as restored and cleansed, the prophet Zephaniah dares to say that God the Father *sings!* "He will joy over thee with singing" (3:17). Our Lord echoed this truth in His parable of the Prodigal Son: "They began to be merry" (Luke 15:24). The father was rejoicing because his son had come home.

But God the Son also sings. He sang a Jewish hymn before He left the Upper Room and went to the cross. Imagine a prisoner on death row singing as he goes to the electric chair or the gas chamber. It was the "joy that was set before him" that helped to strengthen the Savior as He went to the cross (Hebrews 12:2).

On the morning of His resurrection, our Lord sang "in the midst of the congregation" (see Psalm 22:22). The sufferings of the cross were now ended, and He had entered into His glory. His song was a hymn of joyful victory.

God the Holy Spirit sings, and He does it *through God's people who are yielded to Him*. When you and I are filled with the Spirit and filled with the Word (Colossians 3:16), then we have a song to sing that will instruct the saints and glorify the Lord.

Singing is serious business because singing comes from God.

Isaiah 55:1-2
Matthew 4:4
Luke 12:16-21
John 4:31-34

What Are You Eating?

Imagine trying to feed your soul—your inner being—on the things you can store in a barn! But that is just what the farmer in our Lord's parable tried to do, and millions of people today join him in that futile endeavor.

It has well been said that man is a combination of dust and deity. God made us from the earth, but He breathed into us "the breath of life" that can only come from heaven. Mankind has been confused about these two elements ever since our first parents listened to Satan and disobeyed God. Man has been trying to satisfy himself with the things of earth, and that explains why he is restless and searching.

"Thou has made us for Thyself," wrote Augustine, "and our hearts are restless until they rest in Thee."

The only "food" that satisfies the inner person is the truth of the Word of God. Man must eat physical food, or he will die; but he dare not live "by bread alone" (Matthew 4:4). If he tries to live on a diet of "things" and "thrills," he will be dissatisfied and defeated. If he includes in his diet the Word of God, he will find satisfaction and victory.

The Word of God reveals the will of God, and the will of God is the nourishment of the soul. Jesus found His satisfaction in doing the will of His Father, and so can we. How foolish it is to spend time and money on things that cannot satisfy!

Are you living on substitutes?

A Love Affair With Life

How tragic it is when people are like cynical King Solomon: they hate life!

Life is a gift from God, a stewardship from His hand. Unless we choose to end our lives—a terrible thought—we must live, and we must determine *how* we shall live.

Solomon hated life because he could not enjoy it or understand it. He tried everything—physical pleasures, philosophical studies, the amassing of wealth, the exercising of power—and none of those things satisfied him. He erected great buildings and planted lovely gardens, but found no lasting enjoyment in the planning, the doing, or the completing of any of those projects.

Why? Because he was looking at life "under the sun" (Ecclesiastes 2:17)—from a human point of view. He had everything in life except the blessing of God.

Peter tells us that we can and should "love life" (1 Peter 3:10). We should enter each day with gratitude to God for all He has given us, and we should use what He has given us for the good of others and the glory of God. Enjoyment apart from God is empty and transient, but enjoyment in God's will is enriching and edifying.

Let's not *waste* our lives, or merely *spend* our lives; let's *invest* our lives in the things that matter most. Only then will we know what it really means to love life and enjoy God.

143

Matthew 4:1-11; 26:47-53
2 Corinthians 10:1-6
Ephesians 6:17-18
Hebrews 4:12

Spiritual Swordsmanship

The Word of God is pictured as a sword, but God's sword is not like the swords men use. Human swords require human power and skill, but God's sword has power in it, and it is wielded by the wisdom and power of the Spirit. Material swords get duller with use, but the sword of the Spirit never dulls. (Sometimes we who try to use it can become spiritually dull! See Hebrews 5:11-14.) Human swords penetrate only the body—and kill; God's spiritual sword penetrates soul and spirit—and brings life!

As Christians, we are in a dangerous spiritual battle. We need spiritual weapons if we are to defend ourselves and defeat the enemy. Jesus used the sword of the Spirit when He confronted Satan in the wilderness, and He won the victory. Peter tried to use a material sword in the Garden, and he was soundly defeated. The weapons of our warfare are not fleshly.

The better we know the Word of God and the more we apply it to our own lives, the easier it will be to wield it in the battles of life. The believer who ignores his Bible is disarmed, and Satan knows it. It takes spiritual weapons to fight spiritual foes, and those weapons must be used in the power of the Holy Spirit.

The Word of God is your sword. Don't leave home without it.

144

Anything But Pray!

Prayer is not only a wonderful privilege, it is a solemn obligation and a serious ministry. Prayer is not a luxury; it is a necessity. You would think that God's children would enjoy talking to the Father, learning from Him, and receiving His gifts. Yet, for some reason, we would rather do anything than pray!

We would rather argue and debate than pray. In Mark 9:14-29 a desperately needy boy was controlled by a demon, and the disciple could not deliver him. Jesus had given them the authority to cast out demons, and yet they failed. Why? Because they had neglected prayer. All of their debating among themselves and with the Pharisees did not restore their power. They needed to pray. It is generally true that the more we pray, the less we will disagree and debate.

Many believers would rather sleep than pray, just like the three disciples in the Garden. Today our Lord is interceding in glory; yet how much time do we take to pray? Too often we are sound asleep in the morning, when we ought to be getting up to talk to the Lord.

Some people are gazing instead of praying. They are so wrapped up in prophecy and future events that they take little or no time to pray about present needs. To be sure, there is a place for prophetic studies, but we must remember that the book of Revelation, a book of prophecy, *closes with prayer*.

What is keeping *you* from your important time of prayer?

It's a Matter of Motives

Motives are extremely important in the Christian life. God is concerned not only with *what* we do, but *why* we do it.

Paul was a man whose life and ministry were directed by truly spiritual motives. He did what he did "for his [Christ's] body's sake" (Colossians 1:24), that is, the church. Paul loved the church and willingly gave himself to plant churches, build them up, and help them solve their problems. He sacrificed and suffered for the sake of the church. Do we follow his example today?

Paul also lived and labored "for the gospel's sake" (1 Corinthians 9:23). He was unwilling to do anything that would hinder the spread of the gospel of Jesus Christ (Philippians 1:12-21). Paul set aside his own preferences and plans so that he might carry the good news of Jesus Christ to the whole Roman world.

But behind it all was the one overruling motive, "for Christ's sake" (2 Corinthians 12:10). This includes and yet transcends every other motive. Paul took pleasure even in trials and afflictions, because he was doing it for the sake of the Savior who loved him and died for him.

Today, let's watch our motives; for right motives help us to build the kind of life that glorifies God.

He is Greater

Three times in these verses our Lord compares Himself to something holy, and then He claims to be *greater*.

He is greater than the Temple (v. 6). In our Lord's day, Herod's Temple was indeed a magnificent edifice, but it had become a den of thieves. The Jewish religion had degenerated into legalistic routine and was in charge of men who, for the most part, knew nothing of the living God or the Savior He had sent to them. God destroyed that Temple, and it has never been rebuilt.

Men tried to destroy the temple of Christ's body, but they failed (see John 2:18-22)! God raised His Son from the dead, gave Him a glorified body, and received Him back into heaven.

Jesus Christ is greater than the prophet Jonah (v. 41). Jesus is the obedient Son of God, whereas Jonah was a disobedient man who rebelled against God. Jonah brought a message of judgment, whereas Jesus brought a message of salvation and hope. Jonah was swallowed by the great fish, but Jesus suffered the agonies of the cross, died, and rose again.

Finally, Jesus is greater than Solomon—in wisdom, wealth, and authority (v. 42). Solomon's sins brought division to his people, but our Lord's obedience has reconciled men to God and men with men. The glory of Solomon has long faded, but the glory of Jesus Christ will abide forever.

Yes, as Priest, Prophet, and King, Jesus Christ is greater.

Overcoming or Overcome?

Because of their faith in Jesus Christ, God's children should be overcomers. When we were born the first time, we were "born losers," but when we were born again through faith in Christ, we were "born winners." We share the victory of Jesus Christ.

To begin with, we have overcome Satan, the great enemy of God and God's people. Satan is the liar, but Jesus is the Truth. Satan is the destroyer, but Jesus is building His church. Satan is identified with the darkness, but Jesus is the Light. Satan is the murderer, but Jesus is the Life. Satan is the thief, but Jesus is the Giver of every gracious and perfect gift. In Christ, we have all that we need to overcome the evil one.

We have also, by faith, overcome the deceivers that Satan sends into the world to lead people astray. The great test is, "What do you think of Jesus Christ? Is He God the Son, come in human flesh?" The false teachers do not believe this confession of faith, although they try to make it appear that they are orthodox.

Christians have also overcome the world, that evil system of life that is around us, society without God and against Christ. How easy it is to admire the world and gradually be conformed to it. When you are born of God, the Spirit within enables you to maintain a position of holy separation so you are not defiled by the world or trapped in its sins.

Today, by faith, be an overcomer!

Confident Christian Living

The word *confidence* is an important one in John's vocabulary. If a Christian lacks confidence before God, he can never have courage before men. Spiritual power is the result of confident Christian living, but how do we acquire this confidence?

Confidence comes from *abiding*. To "abide in Christ" means to be in fellowship with Him and to include Him in every plan and project. Two friends "abide" in their friendship when they talk together, share experiences, love each other, and get to know each other better. It is this kind of communion that we need daily with Jesus Christ. If we do not abide in Him, then we will be ashamed when He appears.

Confidence also come from *obeying*. An obedient heart is a heart that does not condemn: we know we are walking in a way that pleases the Lord. The believer who has a confident heart knows that he can pray in the will of the God and the Father will answer.

Confidence comes from loving God and loving other believers. (The two go together, you know!) Love casts out fear, for how can you fear someone you love, someone who loves you?

Finally, confidence comes from *knowing the Word of God*. When you believe the witness God gives in His Word about His Son, then you can have confidence toward God as you pray.

Confident Christians are consistent and courageous Christians. Will you be one of them today?

On to Perfection

One of the major themes of Hebrews is *spiritual maturity,* going "on to perfection" and growing in the Lord. The late Dr. Donald Grey Barnhouse often said, "The Book of Hebrews was written to the Hebrews to tell them to quit being Hebrews!" The Hebrew Christians who received this letter were experiencing persecution and were tempted to return to their old faith. Like Israel of old, they wanted to "go back" instead of "going on" and claiming their inheritance.

But if the Hebrews returned to the Old Covenant law, that law could not make them perfect. In fact, the law was their "custodian" because of their immaturity (Galatians 3:23-24, RSV*), and as long as they tried to live under the law, they would remain babes. The law makes nothing perfect because the law is temporary, preparing the way for Christ.

The priesthood was an important part of that legal system, and the priesthood could not bring perfection. Why? Because it, too, was temporary, and the sacrifices the priests offered could never touch the heart or the conscience of the worshipers. No amount of legal obedience or religious sacrifice can of itself produce spiritual maturity.

The exalted Son of God, our High Priest in heaven, is the only One who can lead us into maturity. He works in us to accomplish His will and to conform us to His image. As we worship Him, pray, meditate on the Word, and obediently yield to His Spirit, the Great Shepherd transforms us, and we "go on to perfection" through Him.

*Revised Standard Version.

God Receives the Glory

Peter was obeying the Lord's commandment and letting his light shine. He and John were on their way to a prayer meeting, but even that did not keep them from noticing the cripple and wanting to help. They were unlike the priest and Levite in Christ's parable, who callously passed by "on the other side" (Luke 10:30-37). Peter and John stopped and shared Christ's healing power with the crippled beggar.

But Peter was careful to give God the glory and to use the event as an opportunity to present Jesus Christ. Paul did the same thing in Lystra when the crowd wanted to treat Barnabas and him like gods. What a temptation to take glory for ourselves *even while we are serving the Lord!* Every Christian must overcome that subtle temptation, especially those who are in places of public ministry.

King Herod did just the opposite: he fell for the flattery of the crowd and, as a result, lost his life. (If today God killed everyone who committed this same sin, how many of us would remain living?) Herod succumbed to Satan's lie, "Ye shall be as gods" (Genesis 3:5). Even his high position did not protect Herod from God's judgment. His pride led him to destruction.

As you serve Jesus Christ today, be sure that He receives all the glory. We are but the tools that He uses, and our satisfaction ought to be found in seeing our Lord receive the glory that is due Him.

John 16:33
Romans 12:1-2
James 1:27
1 John 2:15-17

What in the World?

When Jesus warned His disciples about "the world," He was referring to "society organized against God." The world system that is around us, visible and invisible, can pressure us into becoming something other than what God wants us to be, and that usually happens in stages.

First, there is *friendship* with the world. We become interested in what the world is doing and what it has to offer. Before long, we find ourselves *spotted* by the world. Just a spot here and there, but we have been defiled.

When the world sees that we have been spotted, it begins paying attention to us, and then it is easy for us to start *loving* the world. (How often friendship leads to love!) That means that we begin to become cool in our love toward God and in our obedience to His Word, and we begin living for the passing things of time instead of the permanent things of eternity.

In the next step we become *conformed to* the world—and no one can tell the difference. We become like that which we love, and the spots have transformed us.

Jesus Christ has overcome the world. Don't allow the world to overcome you. Let God transform your mind, and the world will not pressure you into conformity.

Under His Wings

The phrase "under his wings" gives many people the mental picture of a mother hen protecting her brood (Matthew 23:37), but that is probably not what the phrase means. The Jews were familiar with the Tabernacle and Temple, and "under his wings" would remind them of the Mercy Seat that sat on the Ark of the Covenant in the Holy of Holies.

The Ark of the Covenant was a wooden chest covered with gold. In it were the tables of the law, and on it was a gold lid called the Mercy Seat. At either end were images of two angelic beings, their wings overshadowing the Mercy Seat. Therefore, to be "under his wings" means to dwell in the very Holy of Holies, in the presence of God, surrounded by His grace and glory.

The Mercy Seat was God's "throne of grace" in the nation of Israel. This was where God met His people and communicated His will to them. Once a year the high priest sprinkled the blood of the sacrifice on the Mercy Seat, covering the law that the people so often disobeyed.

In Jesus Christ, we have our Mercy Seat. The blood has been shed once and for all, and we have access into God's presence (Hebrews 4:14-16; 10:17-22). We can dwell "under his wings" no matter where we are or what our circumstances may be. "Under his wings" is a place of safety, security, and submission. It is also a place of fellowship and enjoyment, where we worship God and adore Him.

No matter where you are today, dwell "under his wings."

Romans 12:10
Hebrews 13:1-2
1 Peter 4:9
2 John

Angels or Devils?

In the days of the early church, there were not many places where a traveling believer could safely spend the night; so the ministry of Christian hospitality was extremely important. Some of these visitors might be itinerant preachers or evangelists, whereas others might be the victims of persecution, fleeing for their lives. The people of God were expected to open their homes to one another and to help each other along the way.

When Abraham entertained some visitors, he discovered that they were two angels *and the Lord Jesus Christ!* The two angels then went to Sodom to visit Lot and to rescue him from judgment (Genesis 18-19). If we share what we have with believers who need us, God will turn them into "angels" of blessing. (The word *angel* means "messenger.") How often loving Christian hospitality has brought special blessing into the home!

But we must beware lest our hospitality give encouragement to the wrong kind of people and compromise our witness. Christians should be kind even to their enemies, but our hospitality can be misunderstood as an endorsement of false doctrine. We dare not entertain *devils* unawares!

Get Ready for a Harvest

The author of Psalm 129 identified with the trials of the nation of Israel. He pictured those trials as deep furrows that were plowed in their backs by their enemies. You can almost feel the pain as you read. In this psalm, the writer gives us some guidelines that we can follow when we find ourselves experiencing affliction.

To begin with, he tells us to *expect affliction.* Peter warns us not to be surprised when the fiery trial comes, because it is an appointed part of the Christian life. To the believer, this world is a battleground, not a playground.

But the psalmist also tells us to *benefit from affliction.* He compares suffering to the furrows the farmer plows in his field. Why does he plow? *Because he is getting ready for a harvest!* You and I can have a harvest of blessing from suffering if we will plant the right seeds. If we plant self-pity, unbelief, and complaining, we will not reap a harvest of blessing; but if we plant faith, hope, and love, the harvest will come.

Finally, the psalmist tells us to *leave the judging to God.* Let God settle the accounts, in His time and in His way. Those who make life difficult for us will in the end reap a small harvest, whereas we will have the privilege of receiving God's blessing and being a blessing to others.

If you feel the plow today, plant the right seeds and trust God for a harvest.

Exodus 40:34
1 Samuel 4:21
2 Chronicles 7:1-3
Ezekiel 9:3; 10:18; 11:23

Ichabod

When Moses dedicated the Tabernacle, the glory of God moved in to dwell with His people. One of the privileges Israel had was that of having "the glory" as their very own (Romans 9:4). But the people sinned and God had to write over the Tabernacle "Ichabod—the glory has departed."

When Solomon dedicated the Temple, God's glory came once again to dwell with His people. History repeated itself: the people turned from God to idols, and the glory had to depart. Ezekiel watched the glory of God depart from the Temple and the city, and then both the Temple and the city were destroyed by the Babylonians.

But God's glory returned to earth in the person of Jesus Christ, the Son of God. "The Word was made flesh, and dwelt [tabernacled] among us . . . and we beheld his glory . . ." (John 1:14). What did men do to that glory? They blasphemed it, saying that His power came from Satan, and then they nailed that glory to a cross.

Where is the glory today? *In the hearts and lives of God's people,* those who have trusted Jesus Christ. Our bodies are His temple, and they should be used to glorify God (1 Corinthians 6:19-20). How we care for our bodies, how we dress, and what we do with our bodies can reflect the glory of God.

Don't end up with "Ichabod" for a name!

Firstborn

In the Bible, the term *firstborn* means more than "born first." It carries with it the idea of honor and superiority. In a Jewish family, the firstborn son received twice as much as the other sons, because he was the special heir. God called the nation of Israel His "firstborn" (Exodus 4:22), because it was special to Him.

Jesus was indeed Mary's firstborn son, for she had never had any children. Our Lord's birth was a miracle birth, for Mary was a virgin when God chose her to be the mother of our Lord (Isaiah 7:14; Luke 1:26-38). But Jesus is the Firstborn in another sense in that He is the highest of all. Jesus is preeminent.

As the "firstborn of all creation," Jesus is prior to creation because He created all things. In fact, they were created by Him and for Him, and He holds all of creation together. He Himself was not created, for He is eternal God. Because men have rejected Him, they have ruined creation, and we are watching things fall apart.

He is the "firstborn from the dead." He is not the first one ever raised from the dead, but He is the greatest and highest of those who have been raised. He raised Himself (John 10:17-18), and He can never die again. Those who trust Jesus Christ never need to fear death, for He is the supreme Victor over death and the grave.

Best of all, He is the "firstborn among many brethren." *This means that one day all believers will be like Christ!* He is the head of the new creation, and if you have been born again, one day you will be like Jesus Christ, the Firstborn. Hallelujah!